London & The Home Counties Poets

Edited by Justine Horne

 Young **Writers**

First published in Great Britain in 2008 by:
Young Writers
Remus House
Coltsfoot Drive
Woodston
Peterborough
PE2 9JX
Telephone: 01733 890066
Website: www.youngwriters.co.uk

SB ISBN 978-1 84431 773 8

Foreword

Young Writers' Big Green Poetry Machine is a showcase for our nation's most brilliant young poets to share their thoughts, hopes and fears for the planet they call home.

Young Writers was established in 1990 to nurture creativity in our children and young adults, to give them an interest in poetry and an outlet to express themselves. Seeing their work in print will encourage them to keep writing as they grow, and become our poets of tomorrow.

Selecting the poems has been challenging and immensely rewarding. The effort and imagination invested by these young writers makes their poems a pleasure to enjoy reading time and time again.

Contents

Brockswood Primary School, Hemel Hempstead

Compton Primary School, Compton

Edenbridge Primary School, Edenbridge

Saffron Watfa (10)   32
Harry Southall (10)   32
Jodi Sky McLaren (9)   33
Rylee William Elsdon (7)   33
Billy-Mark Brooker (7)   33
Robbie Whitaker (9)   33
Riley Smith (11)   34
Jamie Agate (11)   34
Lauren Chilcott (10)   35
Phoebie Leppard-Howard (8)   35
Oliver Irving (11)   36
Molly Walker (11)   36

Gosbecks Primary School, Colchester
Ciara Davies (10)   37

Iwade Community Primary School, Iwade
Bethany Colhoun (9)   37
Amy Fearn (9)   37
Megan L Baker (8)   38
Hannah Dennis (8)   38
Haydn St Pierre (10)   39
Rebecca Alice Whitehead (9)   39
Diana Rufai-Shittu (10)   40
Frankie Brown (10)   40
Jessica Saussus (10)   41
Nneka Igbedioh (9)   41
Louis Coomber (10)   42
Dominic Kisnorbo (10)   42
Leah Marie Rose Sharpe (10)   43
Molly Charlesworth (10)   43
Lauren Preston (10)   44
Laura Gilmour (10)   44
Nicole Marshall (10)   45
Hannah Smith (10)   45
Eleanor Young (9)   46
Lily Taylor (9)   46

John Mayne CE Primary School, Biddenden
Matthew Claydon (8)   47
Rosie May Matthews (9)   48

Knaphill School, Knaphill

Leigh Primary School, Leigh

Luton Junior School, Chatham

St John's Beaumont School, Old Windsor

Nikhil Sharma (11)	65
Christian Taee (9)	66
James Mainwaring (8)	66
Robert Cook (11)	66
Jack Spink (9)	67
Charles Boileve (9)	67
Thomas Martins da Silva (9)	68
Ryan Shum ((10)	68
Harry Chan (9)	69
Oliver Smith (9)	69
Ian Yorke (9)	70
Alessandro Tenconi (9)	70
Max Cunningham (9)	71
Henry Gray (9)	71

St John's CE School, Middlesex

Marcus Thevarajan (8)	71
Cherise Jarrett (8)	72
Alana Gaglio (8)	72
Michelle Gowrialnathan (7)	72
Maximilian Mollenhauer-Starkl (8)	73
Nathan Ferguson (8)	73
Darryl Giffts-Walker (7)	73
Rosh Emmanuel (8)	74
Joseph Brady (8)	74
Blyth McPherson (8)	74
Joelle Phua (8)	75

Sacred Heart Primary School, Battersea

Hanna Touhami (10)	75
Freddy Eytle (10)	75
Courtney Greaves (10)	76
Esther Nkwusi (10)	76
Dominic James McCoy (10)	77
Thomas Maton (10)	77
Marco Minoletti (10)	78
Thomas Smith (9)	78
Louis Wright (10)	78
Rachelle Anera Ogello (9)	79
Nicole Agyekurn (9)	79
Ethan Laurent (10)	79

Amani Clarke (9)	80
Araba Mercer Banson (10)	80
Radhika Nagar (10)	80
Oliwia Jaruzel (10)	80
Victor Kopp (10)	81
Charles Hill (10)	81
Steven Da Silva (10)	81
Reiss Ormonde Cunningham (10)	82

The Grey House School, Hartley Wintney

Angharad Eburne (10)	82
Reuben Chasey (9)	82
Grace Gratwick (11)	83
Saskia Chandler (11)	83
Rishi Shah (10)	84
Verity Jackson (9)	84
Henry Cummings (9)	85
Natasha Lee (10)	85
Joseph Allen (9)	85
Aaron Ueckermann (11)	86
Hannah Byrne (10)	86
Robert Cootes (9)	87
James Myland (8)	87
Holly Smith (10)	88
Jack Shemwell (10)	88
Barnaby Ridley (9)	89
Rory Bertuzzi-Glover (10)	89
Anoushka Chandler (9)	90

The Hill Primary School, Caversham

Ross Hayden (10)	90
Amy Lewis (11)	90
Jonathon Venner (11)	91
Alex Hamilton (11)	91
Andrew McDonald (11)	92
Nicole Lai (11)	92
Beri Wasylciw (11)	93
Zoe Wright (11)	93
Dan Smith (11)	94
Lewis Jenkins (10)	94
Daniel Tanner (11)	94

Sarah Eley (11)	95
Jack Gordon (10)	95
Hannah Wetten	96
Jessica Bradbury (11)	96
Becky Beech (11)	97
Chiara Sexton (10)	97
Daisy Smith (10)	98
Djuna Mount (10)	98
Kayleigh Phillipps (11)	99
Cally Beale-Fletcher (11)	99
Daniella Luff (11)	100
Stephen Barr (11)	100
Morgan Lucie Field (10)	101
Sam Jones (11)	101
Harry Baxter (11)	102

Uxendon Manor Primary School, Kenton

Brandon Lee Worth (10)	102
Janvi Patel (8)	103
Hawa Bati (10)	103
Vivetha Vigineswaran (10)	104
Fawaz Muhsin (10)	104
Tulsi Patel (10)	105
Kelsey Pye (10)	105
Nyveka Sasitharan (8)	106
Katie Hostettler (10)	106
Michael Mason (10)	106
Sanchit Agreawal (9)	107
Kulvinder Wariabharaj (11)	107
Husain Kalimi (7)	108
Tanzim Ahmed (10)	108
Uzayr Undre (9)	109
Laith Elzubaidi (10)	109
Pareena Shah (10)	110
Somil Parmar (10)	110
Diva Patel (10)	111
Keval Mawji (9)	111
Aashni Patel (10)	112
Sania Mallal (9)	112
Nimit Dodhia (9)	113

Wessex Primary School, Maidenhead

Connor Fogarty (10)	113
Shannon Bett (10)	114
Holly Johnson (11)	114
Matthew Sadlier (11)	115
Aiysha Ali (11)	116
Molly Miles (11)	116
Louise Clarke (11)	117
Shannon Hawkins (11)	117
Andrew Newlyn (10)	117
Sakshi Raizada (11)	118
Joshua Belton (11)	118
Julia Reid (11)	119
Zakhia Hussain (11)	119
Kimberley Bradfield (11)	120
Hou-Yee Cheung (11)	120
Ross Moloney (11)	121
Reanne Hawkins (11)	121
Grace Perfect (11)	122
Erin Harley & Jessie Haines (10)	122
Robert Pratley (11)	123
Saima Ali (10)	123
Oliver Crockett & Oliver Mulley (10)	124
Heather Armstrong (11)	124
Alicia Carrington (10)	125
Daisy Fox	125
Hannah Higgins	126
Jack Brinsden (11)	126
Harry Simmonds	127
Catherine Styles (11)	127
Leyan Yucel (11)	128
Hannah Risk (11)	128
Adam Garston (10)	128
Rachel Hibberd (11)	129
Aicha Traore (10)	129
Jenny Barnard (11)	129
Emma Brown (11)	130
Kallum Harris	130
Declan Feltimo (10)	130
Dylan Brownlie	131

West Horndon Primary School, Brentwood

Rebecca Burman (10)	131
Shaun Duggan (9)	131
Phoebe Hardcastle (11)	132
Daisy Bird (10)	132
Amba Davies (9)	132
Toby Lewis-Burrell (11)	133
Kiera Herbert (10)	133
Emily Monk (7)	133
Jordan Shelvey (9)	134
Katie Smith (10)	134
Antoinette Pieri (7)	134
Anya Carter (7)	135
Chloe Oughton (9)	135
Jack Simon & Jo Nann (10)	135
Reece Carter (9)	136
Matthew Scammell (8)	136
Annabel Jarvis (10)	137
Jack Little (11)	137
George Wise (8)	137
Melanie Sedge (9)	138
Alex Oughton (10)	138

Wildridings Primary School, Bracknell

James Hemington (11)	139
Alice Morgan (11)	139
Connor Langham (11)	140
Tyler Jones (10)	140
Kenesha Barracliffe (11)	141
Abigail Harris (11)	141

Woolton Hill Primary School, Newbury

Zara Ryan (9)	142
Ruby Hornsby (9)	142
Edwin Edwards (10)	143
Thomas Hall (10)	143

The Poems

Fire

Fire in the jungle,
Fire in the street,
Fire in the body makes my heart beat.

Fire in my life,
Fire in my dreams,

Fire makes the heart beat faster,
It makes the children scream with laughter,
Fire is true beauty,
Fire is true pain,
Fire in my life makes me insane!

Fire in the fairy tales,
Fire in the eyes,
Because fire makes the world go round,
It makes us live and die,
But fire with the selfish people makes me think *oh no!*

But mainly there is fire in my kitchen
When my grandma cooks a roast,
Or when a very silly person sometimes burns the toast!

Bonnie Bleu Beckett (10)

Go Away

Pollution, pollution go away,
Stop those cars and go and play.

Disease, disease go away,
Help those people stop sneezing today.

War, war go away,
Stop people fighting every day.

Love and peace, don't go away.

Jasmine Norton (11)
Aldermaston CE Primary School, Aldermaston

A Precious Panda

The panda is an endangered creature,
With every adorable little feature.
We must protect them the best we can,
From Earth's horrible poachers known as Man.
The panda is an animal that likes to eat wild bamboo,
But they can't eat it like that if they live in a cruel, caged zoo,
For poor little pandas cause no harm
To the people that live on a bamboo farm.

Katy Styling (11)
Aldermaston CE Primary School, Aldermaston

State Of The Planet

Hurricanes and floods spread out, and gales, all those disasters.
The environment struggles to keep itself together without plasters.
There can be times when you are selfish and in a bad mood.
You can change those times and help not to be rude.
We can save our planet, there's so much that can be done
With support from everyone.
Let's do it, we know how and the time to act is now.

Hazel Gregory (8)
Aldermaston CE Primary School, Aldermaston

The World Gives A Warning

We all care about the world,
So let's make a little difference now,
Animals and people will be in despair if you don't help,
Things will happen like floods, so be aware,
If you don't do anything the world will get a scare.

Lucy Jane Brown (11)
Aldermaston CE Primary School, Aldermaston

The Rainforest

Our rainforests are being cut down,
It's making the animals frown,
Man is killing the monkeys, the snakes and the birds,
It is the worst thing I have ever heard.

We need the trees to live,
Without them we cannot breathe,
The rainforests are more beautiful with the animals in than out.
Man must stop cutting our trees down without a doubt.

Holly Austin (9)
Aldermaston CE Primary School, Aldermaston

Pandas

Top of the near-extinction list,
They really feel the human fist.
While their homes are being crushed,
Most of their families are also shushed.
These black and white cuties are dying out
It is now the humans' turn to help!
Put down your guns and tools of death
Go and stop your life of theft.

Jack Hardiman (8)
Aldermaston CE Primary School, Aldermaston

Elephant

Elephants are endangered creatures,
They get hunted down for their wonderful tusks.
Their trunk is long and wiggly.
Elephants' feet are big and clompy.
An elephant's tail is swishy and swirls about.
Their ivory tusks are pointy and sharp.

Annabel Ford (11)
Aldermaston CE Primary School, Aldermaston

The Woodland Rap

This is the rhythm
Of the woodland rap
Trees go whoosh
And twigs go snap
Mud is mush
Branches go zap
When you do the rhythm
Of the woodland rap
Wheeeeeee!

It's the woodland rap
It's filled with air
Give yourself a shake up
If you dare
Stamp your feet
On the dirty floor
Let's do the woodland rap
Once more.

This is the rhythm
Of the woodland rap
Birds go tweet
And woodpeckers tap
Animals eat
And wings go flap
When you do the rhythm
Of the woodland rap
Wheeeeeee!

It's the woodland rap
It's filled with air
Give yourself a shake up
If you dare
Stamp your feet
On the dirty floor
Let's do the woodland rap
Once more.

This is the rhythm
Of the woodland rap
Badgers go bop
And foxes go clap
Rabbits go hop
And little mice nap
When you do the rhythm
Of the woodland rap
Wheeeeeee!

Abigail Spoor (9)
Aldermaston CE Primary School, Aldermaston

Worldwide Troubles

Litter is everywhere,
It decides to take flight,
It goes around everywhere,
Wind blows it, even at night.

Many animals are killed,
Throughout the world,
Humans are the killers,
Around the whole wide world.

Disease is horrible,
It makes people ill,
They catch it from animals or dirty water,
All they need is a pill,
But people in Africa,
Can't help being ill.

Ricky Hutchins (10)
Aldermaston CE Primary School, Aldermaston

The Wildlife Rap

This is the rhythm
Of the wildlife rap
Where cows go *moo*
And woodpeckers *tap*
Streams are blue
And twigs go *snap*
When you're doing the rhythm
Of the wildlife rap
Ssshhhhh!

It's the wildlife rap
And it's a scare
Give yourself a shake-up
On your walk to school
Put your hiking boots on
And step out your door
And let's do the wildlife rap
Once more.

This is the rhythm
Of the wildlife rap
Flowers have power
And they taste quite sour
Luggage goes *clink*
And cups go *tap*
When you're doing the rhythm
Of the wildlife rap.

It's the wildlife rap
And it's a scare
Give yourself a shake-up
On your walk to school
Put your hiking boots on
And step out your door
And let's do the wildlife rap
Once more.

This is the rhythm
Of the wildlife rap
When frogs are leaping
And fish go *flap*
Willows are weeping
And branches go *clap*
When you're doing the rhythm
Of the wildlife rap
Ssshhhh!!

Nicolle York (9)
Aldermaston CE Primary School, Aldermaston

Litter And Dirt

Looking across the abandoned Earth,
Nothing is left but litter and dirt.
No birds are singing,
No abused animals hurt,
Nothing is left but litter and dirt.
No trees stand tall,
No people at all,
No animals are left to hurt,
Nothing is left but litter and dirt.

Cristina Carreňo (11)
Aldermaston CE Primary School, Aldermaston

The Wildlife Poem

W ater whooshes
I nsects encounter
L ife listens
D ormice dream
L adybirds lift off
I guanas evolve
F ish flap
E arth erupts.

Stéphane Howard Charles Morris (10)
Aldermaston CE Primary School, Aldermaston

The Woodland Rap

This is the rhythm
Of the woodland rap,
Trees are swaying
And twigs go *snap,*
Leaves are laying,
Bird wings flap,
When you're doing the rhythm
Of the woodland rap,
Whooooshh!

These are the sounds
Of the woodland rap,
Birds go *tweet,*
And foxes' feet *tap,*
Rabbits thump their feet
When badgers do their daily lap,
Let's carry on with the
Woodland rap.

These are the sights
Of the woodland rap,
Trees are brown,
See the beavers clap,
The foxes give a frown
And otters take a nap,
When you see the sights
Of the woodland rap,
Whooooshh!

This is the rhythm
Of the woodland rap,
Trees are swaying
And twigs go *snap,*
Leaves are laying
Bird wings flap,
When you're doing the rhythm
Of the woodland rap,
Whooooshh!

This is the rhythm
Of the woodland rap,
Trees are creaking,
Twigs go clap,
Mice are squeaking
Whilst sitting babies on their lap,
When you're doing the rhythm
Of the woodland rap,
Whooooshh!

Amy Hardiman (9)
Aldermaston CE Primary School, Aldermaston

Litter Should Be Banned

Litter should be banned
It will mess up the streets.
Litter should be banned
It makes our lives a terrible mess.
Litter should be banned
It will end up causing pollution.
It will ruin our community.
Litter should be banned.
Litter should be banned!

Rhian Taylor (8)
Aldermaston CE Primary School, Aldermaston

Litter

You need to clean the litter up
You need to clean it up fast
Because if you clean the litter up
You will win a prize.
Dirty, dusty and horrible
You really don't want to do it,
But you have to get rid of it.

Somer Lewese Jordan (7)
Aldermaston CE Primary School, Aldermaston

The Animal Rap

This is the rhythm
Of the animal rap
Chicks go *squeak*
And birds go *flap*
Owls take a peek
Woodpeckers *tap*
This is the rhythm
Of the animal rap.

It's the animal rap
And bunnies bounce
The deer run and leap
And foxes pounce,
Baby lambs sleep,
A horse stamps once
Look at the movement
Of the animal rap.

This is the rhythm
Of the animal rap
Badgers are stripy
And beetles are black
Slugs are slimy
And puppy dogs yap
When you're doing the rhythm
Of the animal rap.

Jon Grieve (9)
Aldermaston CE Primary School, Aldermaston

Litter

You need to clean the litter up.
You need to do it fast,
Otherwise the animals will cry out fast.
You need to get your plastic bags and stop stuffing them full,
Then the Earth will be shining clean, *cool, cool, cool!*

Emily Faulkner (8)
Aldermaston CE Primary School, Aldermaston

The Woodlands Rap

This is the rhythm
Of the woodlands rap,
Trees are swaying
And twigs go snap,
Hens are laying
And birds go *flap,*
When you're doing the rhythm
Of the woodlands rap,
Wssshhh!

It's the woodlands rap
And it's a fright,
Give a bush a shake-up
When it's night,
Rattle your teeth
And don't break the law,
And let's do the woodlands rap
Once more.

This is the rhythm
Of the woodlands rap,
Horses' hooves *clink*
And woodpeckers *tap,*
Dead bones sink
And trees give sap,
When you're doing the rhythm
Of the woodlands rap.
Wssshhh!

It's the woodlands rap
And it's a scare,
Give yourself a shake-up
If you see a bear,
Rattle your teeth
And don't break the law,
And let's do the woodlands rap
No more.

Max Barlow (9)
Aldermaston CE Primary School, Aldermaston

Woodland Rap

This is the rhythm
Of the woodland rap,
Rabbits go hop,
Beetles go snap,
Horses' hooves clap,
Birds go flap,
When you're doing the rhythm
Of the woodland rap,
Whoooosh!

It's the woodland rap
And it's a scare,
Give a bush a shake up
If you dare,
Put on your wellies,
Breathe fresh air
And let's do the woodland rap
With care,
These are the colours of the woodland rap,
Leaves are green,
Brown bears nap,
Near the blue stream
Red squirrels tap,
When you're doing the rhythm
Of the woodland rap,
Whooooosh!

Callum Boyden (9)
Aldermaston CE Primary School, Aldermaston

Litter

Litter, litter spoils the nature reserves.
Litter, litter isn't that helpful for the future world.
Litter, litter is horrible.

What do you think of the world?

Eleanor Mott (8)
Aldermaston CE Primary School, Aldermaston

Rainforest Leaves

Ripping down rainforest leaves
This is bad, stop it please.
All the animals will soon be dead,
So stop before they lose their heads.
The rainforest will soon be gone
Staring up at the moon,
Wishing it will all be good soon.
The rainforest is a precious thing,
We all should not ruin it please!
We all need it so we should all pull our weight,
Before it's too late.
Before all the animals have a date with extinction!
So stop pulling down the rainforest leaves.

Olivia Woollam (11)
Aldermaston CE Primary School, Aldermaston

Help

Poverty, poverty please go away
Let children have a home and food to eat
Poverty, poverty please go away
Let them have clean water not dirty, oh please
Poverty, poverty please go away
Give them clean water without any disease
Poverty, poverty they need your help now
Poverty, poverty don't let them suffer.

Gemma Moore (11)
Aldermaston CE Primary School, Aldermaston

Battle

Battle is red
The soldiers are dead

The homes are no more
So the people are poor

The plants are blown up
So is the cup

Some people are sad
Others extremely mad

People are dying
While others are lying.

Elliot Jones (8)
Aldermaston CE Primary School, Aldermaston

Litter

If you throw litter
You won't feel better.
If you throw litter on the floor
People will call you names from their door.
If you throw litter on the floor
People will make you go far away.

So throw your litter in the bins
And pick up the tins.
Then people will not poke you like a pin.
The landfill will be full
And it will be hard to clean.

Mubashirah Saleem (8)
Al-Falah Primary School, Clapton

Homeless

I am poor and have no more.
I ask people and beg people.
I sleep next to a bin
And I do not have a house.
I need money to buy some honey
'Can I have a couple of pence to buy something?' I ask.
But they call me names
And they kick me in my face!
And that's very painful.

Izzadeen Brooks (9)
Al-Falah Primary School, Clapton

Racism Is Wrong

R emember racism
A frican people
C an't stop crying
 I t's so cruel
S imple death in three seconds
M urder of racism

Just remember!

Liam Gardner (10)
Bobbing Village School, Sittingbourne

The Tiger

Tiger, your green eyes
Will they switch off and die
Or are you going to run away?
Will you go today or Tuesday?
My dad says it's us
Please don't go on the bus
We can stop it before the bullet hits!

Luke Adaka (11)
Bobbing Village School, Sittingbourne

Recycling!

R abbits dying nearly every day.
E lephants getting stuck in things.
C ats crying for help.
Y ou are doing all this to animals.
C ars sending pollution in the air.
L itter needs to be *stopped,*
I nside and out.
N asty things are happening to animals.
G uilty, guilty are you for dropping all this litter.

Recycling!

Georgia Ferdinand (11)
Bobbing Village School, Sittingbourne

Recycling Rubbish

R ubbish
E co-friendly
C limate change
Y ou drop litter
C aring for our world
L itter
I magine a better place
N ice environment
G row up in a better world.

Eloise Frankham (10)
Bobbing Village School, Sittingbourne

Endangered Ones! - Haiku

Whales are everywhere,
Dolphins are even cared for,
Endangered, but why?

Beckie Foster (10)
Bobbing Village School, Sittingbourne

Children In Poverty

There is a girl named Charly
She lives in poverty
She was born in poverty
She will die in poverty
Will poverty ever end for Charly?
Charly is three
Ten million children die every year before their fifth birthday
Will this be her?
Will she be one of those children?
I hope not.
Vaccinations could save her
Though she can't afford them
There is food all around her
She can't afford that either
She could live but she won't.
Make the difference and help her please.

Lois Wakefield (11)
Bobbing Village School, Sittingbourne

Pure Perfection

If you get stopped on the street,
By some people who want to eat,
Don't just carry on and say no,
Give them some money and then you can go.

How would you feel without a home?
You'd be so hurt and so alone,
Now please show some clean affection,
And help our world become pure perfection.

Natalie Towers (11)
Bobbing Village School, Sittingbourne

Would You Like To Be In My Shoes?

We think you're rich
In your developed world
With food, clothes and nutrition

My child died as well as the 153 million under the age of five.
My world has *no* vitamins
Because I am in one of the 54 countries who cannot provide food.

Is there no escape?
The sun beats down on my head
Burning since I have no protection.

You hear mums crying
They have lost someone close
I would like to be in your shoes.

I want it to stop
Would you like to be in my shoes?

Kirsty Sayers (11)
Bobbing Village School, Sittingbourne

The Life Of A Dolphin

I awake to the sound of boats
Evil boats that crush us
Boats that kill and savage us
Their nets tangle us
Then we die of suffocation

Next oil comes seeping down
Polluting the ocean
We cough, we splutter
As the oil poisons us
As the oil kills us.

Jessica Daly (11)
Bobbing Village School, Sittingbourne

Me And My Doorway Prison

I live in a doorway prison
My home is here
My home is there
My home is everywhere and nowhere
My holey jumper and dirty old jeans
Are all I have
I carry my life around
All I have are newspapers to keep me warm
But I still sleep on a stone-cold floor
For food I have everything and nothing
Do you care?
Do you realise?
Help me.
If you need me I'll be in my doorway prison!

Bethany Joy Thurston (11)
Bobbing Village School, Sittingbourne

Thoughts Of A Tiger

My teeth are
White as white
They reflect the sun
Like a light.

When I jump out
You may get a fright
But you'll be alright.

All my hair is falling
Off everywhere.

Don't forget I have feelings!

Adam Bergin (10)
Bobbing Village School, Sittingbourne

Hungry

We're all in Third World places in some way,
Some better, some worse.
We have no water, food or home,
We wish we had a life like you,
With food, water and a home.
We starve in the boiling sun, only rags to wear,
These hardly keep us from the sun's deadly rays,
This means death is only a few years away.
Some people in our Third World countries would chop
off their right arm for food!

I hope this poem has taught you something about Third World
Countries and in future you *will* help them.

Roland Somorin (11)
Bobbing Village School, Sittingbourne

Life Of A Panda

Hi, my name is Lily the panda,
That's right, a panda.
Pandas are just amazing.
We live till we are thirty years old.
People think that we are boring
But they are wrong.
We are kind to your friends and family.

So can you help us?
Will you be able to help the environment
And look after our world?
If you do, we will be happy to help you more.

Stevie-Elise Atkins (11)
Bobbing Village School, Sittingbourne

Homeless

Homeless is what they call us,
They say we have no home,
Just because we live on the streets.

But homeless may be what we are.
Living out on the streets,
Who knows? Maybe it is.
But what about people and kids?

So I hope you understand how we feel,
We don't live like you,
Nice and clean and new!

So, now I really wish for the future to come,
So then we won't feel so dirty and numb.
Then people won't call us 'homeless',
So I hope we become just like you.

Lauren Horn (11)
Bobbing Village School, Sittingbourne

Starvation

S tarvation eats the people,
T earing through their souls,
A nd kills all the livestock,
R efilling the death holes.
V illages and towns shell-shocked by disease,
A nd not even the wealthy can escape the fleas.
T aking people and their lives,
I n a force that shocks the archives.
O n this dreadful, lonely day,
N obody cares that they can't play.

Eliot Budgen (11)
Bobbing Village School, Sittingbourne

Extinction

One day I wake up,
The clouds are coming closer,
The dark sky makes me shiver,
As the hunters come marching in.

They chase,
They kill,
I run, I hide,
As the hunters come marching in.

They're strong and mean,
They're bad and cruel,
They're evil and nasty,
These are the hunters that come marching in.

Niamh Flannery (11)
Bobbing Village School, Sittingbourne

Endangered Animals

E ndangered animals due for extinction
N ever to be seen again
D o something about it
A nd help them to be saved, or
N ever will they be seen again
G iant pandas
E verything rare, even the garden
R ed squirrels
E ndangered animals
D o we never want to see them again?

Hannah Crawford (11)
Bobbing Village School, Sittingbourne

Say 'No!'

When your dad says, 'I'll drive you to school,'
Say, 'No!'
When your mum says, 'Just throw it away,'
Say, 'No!'
When your friend says, 'Let's go hunting,'
Say, 'No!'
When the army says, 'Can you fight in the war?'
Say, 'No!'

So please listen to me and say, 'No!'
And make the world a better place.

Ry Tomkins (9)
Brockswood Primary School, Hemel Hempstead

Why Does The World Have To Be Ruined?

Why does the world have to be ruined
By polluted rivers and disease?
Animals are becoming extinct.
Litter is being thrown on the streets.
People are having to go to war to save their countries.
But we can make a difference.
Yes, we children, we can save the planet
So when we grow up we can have a better world to live in.

Alys Chendlik (9)
Brockswood Primary School, Hemel Hempstead

Pollution

Wasting rubbish really ruins our planet,
If we recycle, then we children
Will have a better world to live in.

Pollution ruins our planet,
Please walk, don't drive!

Bobbie Healy (8
Brockswood Primary School, Hemel Hempstead

Help The World

All around the world
The streets are littered.
In rivers and canals
Litter causes pollution.
The fish and the environment suffer,
Help the world!
Help us to have a better place,
Don't forget,
Don't harm animals,
Help the world!

Sasha Gilbey (8)
Brockswood Primary School, Hemel Hempstead

Recycle Today

Birds aren't flying,
They are dying.
Don't throw plastic
Into the Atlantic.
Earth is a great place to stay,
Don't throw rubbish . . .
Recycle today.

Tyrek Richards-Morris (9)
Brockswood Primary School, Hemel Hempstead

Animals Are Dying

Animals are dying
People are crying
Stop dumping plastic in the sea.

Animals are dying
And the world is sighing
Because people are killing elephants.

Thomas Oxland-Isles (8)
Brockswood Primary School, Hemel Hempstead

Animals Are Dying

Animals are dying
Birds are not flying
Because humankind is being mean.

Monkeys and tigers are becoming extinct
And so is the furry little lynx.

People are chopping down trees
From the high sky to their knees
And they do not know what they're doing.

Men are going mad and they're really bad
Chopping and killing all the living things!

Jack Walsh (8)
Brockswood Primary School, Hemel Hempstead

Saving Our Planet

Cars are polluting our world by leaving fumes and smoke.
People are throwing rubbish in the sea.
The rubbish is trapping the animals.
Trees are being chopped down.
People are at war,
We need help to stop,
Please help!

Amy Worrell (8)
Brockswood Primary School, Hemel Hempstead

Look After The World

All around the world is pollution,
Litter and extinction.
We need to recycle more in our homes
And make our world a better place for everyone.

Samuel Gaastra (7)
Brockswood Primary School, Hemel Hempstead

Save The World

Help us save the world
And stop chopping down the trees.

Think of all the animals
And all the birds and bees.

Stop driving cars
And try to walk a lot more.
We need trees
We need oxygen
To help us live a happy life.

Please help us save the world!

Jody Randall (8)
Brockswood Primary School, Hemel Hempstead

Sea Pollution

I have seen teenagers throwing plastic
into the rivers.
I have seen the sea with rubbish
floating on top.
I have seen birds on top of the sea
covered in oil.
I have seen penguins and other creatures
with plastic around their heads.

Stephen Walker (8)
Brockswood Primary School, Hemel Hempstead

Atlantic Penguins

Don't throw plastic can holders into the sea,
Because they will travel to the Atlantic,
Penguins have to swim through them,
Then they become caught
And then they will die.

Chelsea Van Gelder (9)
Brockswood Primary School, Hemel Hempstead

It's Not About Us

What are we doing to our creatures?
All barks and screeches,
They've done nothing wrong,
Not short, nor long.

Some animals are strange,
They come in every range,
Some animals are funny,
They become lively when it's sunny.

Dog, monkey, cat, giraffe,
Dolphin, penguin, pig, calf,
Parrot, chameleon, fish, whale,
Elephant, snake, badger, snail.

So why do we not care?
Just stop and have a stare,
You'll soon realise what's not right,
You'll think about the animals all night.

Georgia Tranter (8)
Compton Primary School, Compton

Pollution

Our world is a wonderful place,
So let's save the human race.
This poem will show you how
To save the world, so read it now!
Recycle all your rubbish and more,
Turn off lights and close the door.

Don't chop down trees,
Or no one will be able to breathe.
So listen up I'm telling you how
To save this world not tomorrow, now!
So work together as a team to find a solution
For the world's despicable pollution.

Emily McEwan (10)
Compton Primary School, Compton

The Eco-Rap

We're the three MCs
Of the Big Green Poetry Machine.
Keepin' the world clean
From the obscene
CO_2.
We need help
Help from you.

Find a bin
And put rubbish in.
Don't use your car
Use your bicycle.
Start to recycle.

Don't cut down trees
Or we won't be able to breathe.
Let's find a solution
Save the world from all this pollution.
Everyone should know
Everyone be eco.

This is from the three MCs
Helping you to save our *planet!*

Oliver Kidby-Hunter, Jason Bint & Kieran Collins (11)
Compton Primary School, Compton

Save The Animals

Our animals are wonderful creatures,
They are big and small with some random features.
Animals out there are dying right now,
So this poem will show you how,
To save these animals,
This risk you should take,
So of yourself you should definitely make,
A strong and brave eco-warrior,
To save the world and make it stronger!

Coral Fountain (10)
Compton Primary School, Compton

Don't Be Mean - Be Green!

The world needs more care,
To save the lions, fish and bear.
Save the animals, big and small,
Stripy zebras and giraffes so tall.
Plant some trees,
We must do all these.
Recycle bottles, paper and cans,
Walk, don't drive cars or vans.
Walk to school,
Save the donkeys, horses and mule.
Don't throw rubbish on the floor,
Turn off lights when you close the door.
Recycle and reuse,
If no, do you know what we might lose?
Stop releasing CO_2,
And the cows will give a happy *moo!*
Keep the world a happy place,
Rather than a big disgrace.
Save water and don't waste fuel,
Helping the planet, it's so cool!
Think about the things you do,
And the world will be good to you!

Bryony Rawstron (10) & Hannah Sanders (11)
Compton Primary School, Compton

Save The World

Come on, it's time to save the world
If we don't work together
We'll kill the world
And if we work together we'll be alright.
We can work this out
Work this
We can work this *oooout!*
Where are we going to save the world?
Where are we going to . . .
Save the world?
We can work this out
Work this
We can work this *oooout!*
But most of all we have to
Save the world . . .
Save it!

Nathan Smith & Harry Franklin (9)
Compton Primary School, Compton

Oh World!

Oh world, oh world,
What's happened to you?
The people who dump stuff are bad too!

Oh world, oh world,
What have people done,
Making pollution and killing the sun?
Oh my God, world,
I don't have a clue,
What's happened to you.

Oh world, oh world
What have people done
Making pollution and killing the sun?

Liam Bint & David Cooper (9)
Compton Primary School, Compton

The Compost Rap

Compost, compost, compost, put it in a compost bin
Apple cores and banana skins, put them in a compost bin.
Now let's move onto global warming, while we think what to do.
Global warming, global warming, the sun's rays are coming through.
All the ice is melting now, it's bad for me and you.
Now moving on to the air, pollution is everywhere,
From cats and dogs, to sheep and frogs, they're choking from the air.
So walk to school,
It could be cool,
Don't drive your car today.
So turn off all your lights today,
And we can save the world!

Rhidian Hill (10) & Robert Parkington (9)
Compton Primary School, Compton

Environment

Greenhouse gases are killing lads and lasses.
Toxic waste turning the air black,
By people burning tarmac.

Global warming getting closer every day.
Cars running their motors, letting off gas,
Aeroplanes adding to this domination,
Keep the air nice and save the nation.

Harvey Snewing (11)
Edenbridge Primary School, Edenbridge

Devastating War

W oeful and wicked
A trocities and abominations
R ampaging and rioting.

Harry Garcia (11)
Edenbridge Primary School, Edenbridge

War Kennings

Country-taker,
Shell-shocker,
Gut-blower,
Church-stealer,
Skin-peeler,
Torture-chamber,
Tank-destroyer,
Time-waster,
Life-taker,
Trench-maker,
Mind-shaker,
Bomb-flinger,
Love-clinger.

George Johnson (11)
Edenbridge Primary School, Edenbridge

Litter

L azy people,
I n their ignorance,
T hrowing litter,
T hrough the air,
E ating food,
R efusing to put it in the bin.

Saffron Watfa (10)
Edenbridge Primary School, Edenbridge

Pollution Kennings

Life-destroyer,
Cancer-causer,
Tree-killer,
Cloud-blackener,
Oxygen-taker.

Harry Southall (10)
Edenbridge Primary School, Edenbridge

Litter Kennings

Can-thrower,
Packet dropper,
Drink-chucker,
Bottle-breaker,
Animal-hurter.

Jodi Sky McLaren (9)
Edenbridge Primary School, Edenbridge

War - Haiku

People die in wars,
Bang! Bang! Five bullets, you're dead!
There are big, bad guns.

Rylee William Elsdon (7)
Edenbridge Primary School, Edenbridge

War - Haiku

Armour, spears and shields,
These days people use rifles,
Always ends in death.

Billy-Mark Brooker (7)
Edenbridge Primary School, Edenbridge

Litter - Haiku

Do not throw litter,
Do not throw cans on the floor,
Because it is bad.

Robbie Whitaker (9)
Edenbridge Primary School, Edenbridge

Environment

E verything and everywhere is changing every day
N ow we have the little ones not noticing the pollution in a way.
V ery many trees are being chopped down,
    just for the factories in the town.
I n our daily lives we ask to stop the destruction against trees.
R ainforests are rare, they keep on getting a scare
    by being chopped down.
O n goes the life of people, trees and creatures suffer tragedy
    all year round.
N ow comes the extinction of animals and trees.
M any are rare like the big, fat, grizzly bear.
E verything is gone now, more houses everywhere,
    less free wild animals getting a scare.
N ot being harmful to others but being kind.
T ill then it'll never be together again.

Riley Smith (11)
Edenbridge Primary School, Edenbridge

Environment

The sun lights up the land,
and a spark of happiness burns my heart,
at the sheer beauty of the planet.
But, under the spectacular rays,
destruction takes place,
then one thousand arrows pierce my heart.
Animals being killed, smoke in the air,
our planet is dying, right before our eyes.
But our generation can stop all this . . .
stop the destruction and save the planet!

Jamie Agate (11)
Edenbridge Primary School, Edenbridge

Environment

Grey clouds are forming,
Pollution is taking over the town,
No one has noticed
What can we do . . . ?

Toxic fumes are everywhere,
People don't care,
Everyone is smoking,
What can we do . . . ?

Changes happen every day,
But not this bad,
Litter is always thrown to the ground,
What can we do . . . ?

People are scared,
Global warming is going to happen,
How can we stop it?
What can we do . . . ?

We are all afraid,
We need people to stop,
We all have the world in our hands,
Can you help us?

Lauren Chilcott (10)
Edenbridge Primary School, Edenbridge

Being Homeless

Being homeless is not fair,
Give your money if you care!
If you see a person on the street,
Give them sweets or food to eat!

Phoebie Leppard-Howard (8)
Edenbridge Primary School, Edenbridge

Environment

Everything
is changing in and
out the day. There used to
be a time when you could see
the trees sway. But now the
trees are dying, they no
longer sway. The children
will now play, but when
they are older they
will realise
that
there
will
be
no
trees
to
play
on!

Oliver Irving (11)
Edenbridge Primary School, Edenbridge

Environment

Rubbish-dropper,
Chewing gum-spitter,
Tree-chopper,
Stream-polluter,
Forest-destroyer,
War-creator,
World-killer.

Molly Walker (11)
Edenbridge Primary School, Edenbridge

Always Recycle

Don't you know you're a terrible drag
If you don't put your plastic in the clear bag?
Haven't you heard it's a terrible sin,
Not to put vegetable waste in a compost bin?
It is extremely important to be seen
Putting cans and bottles in the box that's green.
Not to recycle is a bad disease,
So for the sake of our planet - *recycle, please!*

Ciara Davies (10)
Gosbecks Primary School, Colchester

Recycling

Recycling rubbish is the best thing you can do.
Recycling rubbish helps the environment too.
Recycling rubbish is a cool thing to do.
Makes you feel grown up for the things that you do.
Plastic, glass, paper, cardboard and bottles
Are things you can recycle.
Recycling, recycling is the great thing to do!

Bethany Colhoun (9)
Iwade Community Primary School, Iwade

War

War is painful
War is tough

War is scary
War is rough

War is stressful
War is . . . enough!

Amy Fearn (9)
Iwade Community Primary School, Iwade

A Load Of Rubbish!

It really makes me bitter
When people throw their litter
The world would be a better place
Without this rubbish in my face

I see it on the news
And it really makes me blue
I wish people would care
About the rubbish everywhere

Why are people under an illusion
About all this pollution?
All it causes is disease
When it's carried on the breeze.

Why don't people care?

Megan L Baker (8)
Iwade Community Primary School, Iwade

Homeless

Being homeless is a sad thing to be
because it is a lonely place to be.
Litter is a bad thing to do
because it can harm animals and people too.
War is a dangerous thing
because it can kill people.
Some animals are kind
but some are fierce.
Lots of people get diseases
and animals too.
Rainforests have a lot of animals.

Hannah Dennis (8)
Iwade Community Primary School, Iwade

In This World There Are Wars

In this world there are wars
And they really upset me
So much death and destruction
Why can't people be free?

When I see it on the news
I feel so sad inside
People lose their families
And I feel sorrow for those who died.

If everyone could just make friends
And be peaceful in their ways
Then this world would be a better place
For us to live our days.

Haydn St Pierre (10)
Iwade Community Primary School, Iwade

Who Are You?

Racism makes me feel sad,
I wish I could do something about it,
Black, orange or white,
It's only the colour of their skin.

Stop, stop, stop . . .
How do you feel about it?
One day, it might happen to you,
So don't do it too.

Now, let's all get on,
And enjoy our lives today.
The world would be better
If we all lived peacefully together.

Rebecca Alice Whitehead (9)
Iwade Community Primary School, Iwde

Recycle

R ecycling could stop the pollution from happening,
recycling litter could make the world cleaner.

E xtinction could happen to our lovely animals,
if we don't do something about this problem.

C limate change is becoming a serious problem,
being rainy instead of sunny. *We need to do something.*

Y our litter is changing our world so you *need* to change your ways,
if you take serious action, you will be a life saver.

C learing our world will mean a lot to everyone
and you could be proud of yourself for changing your ways.

L itter is bad for our world, recycling your litter could
change everything.

E veryone could pitch in and save our world
and then we'll live in a lovely world.

Diana Rufai-Shittu (10)
Iwade Community Primary School, Iwade

Recycling

They throw it down upon the ground,
It really makes me angry.
I'm talking about the naughty ones
Who never bin their litter.
How easy it is to separate
The paper from the tin
And then to place them easily
In the recycle bin.
It's good for the environment
It keeps pollution down
It makes the future better
For the people in our town.

Frankie Brown (10)
Iwade Community Primary School, Iwade

Please Don't Kill A Polar Bear

Please don't kill a polar bear
You will be sorry when they are not there
You can stop it happening now
Would you like to know how?

The world is getting hotter
Stop driving in your cars
Walk and use your legs.
Put your washing on the line
And get some use out of your pegs.

If you turn off your TVs
And your lights when you don't need them.
Recycle all your rubbish and put the teabag in the compost bin,
The polar bear will say 'Thank you.'
For not making his home wetter.

Jessica Saussus (10)
Iwade Community Primary School, Iwade

The World Can Be A Better Place
If You Stop Polluting

If you stop polluting, the world can be a better place,
No bad diseases will be flying around,
It will be OK!
You will not hear a single sound.

Now you know how clean the world can be,
Stop littering,
Start recycling,
And the world will be as clean as glitter.

If you follow the instructions,
The world will be good,
You will not believe it,
You will have a clean neighbourhood.

Nneka Igbedioh (9)
Iwade Community Primary School, Iwade

Save Our Future

If you chop down trees
Animals will die.

Don't drop litter
And please don't lie.

Pollution destroys our planet
This we have to stop.

Recycling is one answer
And it doesn't cost a lot.

War is never good
Too many people die.

It kills and injures anyone
Destroying many lives.

So make the world a greener place
So we can save the future of the human race.

Louis Coomber (10)
Iwade Community Primary School, Iwade

Raging Recycling

Paper, plastic, glass and metal,
These are all recyclable.

Paper comes from trees, so tall,
Metal comes from the ground, it's a mineral.

Plastic is made by man's fair hand,
Glass is a mineral made from sand.

If you see them lying around,
Then pick them up off the ground.

Don't be lazy, put them in the bin,
The one that's used for recycling.

Dominic Kisnorbo (10)
Iwade Community Primary School, Iwade

Looking After The Environment

When the grass isn't green,
The animals smell of extinction,
The solution is less cars,
Because the gas is a pollution.

The Earth has its own war
With all the litter,
But we're safe when the weather is bitter,
Because then we don't drop litter.

And so we have to take care
Of the environment,
And think more about the world
And Kent.

Leah Marie Rose Sharpe (10)
Iwade Community Primary School, Iwade

Keep It Tidy!

The world would look much better,
If it were tidy every day.
So by putting our rubbish in a bin,
We would be helping it to stay that way.

It only takes a second,
To pick up a packet or a can,
And makes the job much easier,
For the recycle van.

Recycling is much better,
And so easy for us to do.
So when you think your litter can be used again,
Put it in the bin that's *blue!*

Molly Charlesworth (10)
Iwade Community Primary School, Iwade

Change The World

C ome, help us change the world and make it a better place
H azards such as litter are damaging the world.
A nimals are sadly becoming extinct
N o, you're wrong, it gets worse!
G ases flowing wildly
E nergy used too much

T hese are the things that affect us
H omelessness is very hurtful for some people
E very day in poverty

W ar is really sad
O r selfish in some ways
R eligions cause racism . . .
L ive together in peace
D o help us change the world!

Lauren Preston (10)
Iwade Community Primary School, Iwade

We Are Harming The Animals

The world is heating
Ice is melting
Polar bears and penguins are dying.

The waters are rising
Water creatures are hunted
Fish and whales are dying.

Forests and jungles disappearing
Monkeys and pandas are dying
We love the world, please let's save it!

Laura Gilmour (10)
Iwade Community Primary School, Iwade

In My Car

Sitting in my car, not going far,
There's a sight, a guy on a bike,
Looks like fun, riding in the sun.
No stops at all, while I sit and crawl.
This traffic . . . it makes me sick!
Moving so free . . . that could be me!

Oh nice thought, this car . . . I just bought,
What if I need to go to the mall or make a call?
What about sweat? Surely then I'll regret.
And another thing, what clothes would I bring?

With so much else to do, my life is just a zoo.
Living this way, this is the price I pay,
Sitting in my car, not going far.

Nicole Marshall (10)
Iwade Community Primary School, Iwade

Our World

I love to go to the park,
To smell a fresh oak tree,
To taste the wild strawberries,
To feel the nice cool wind,
To hear the tweeting of the birds,
To see all of the lovely sights.

But when I went to the park this morning,
Everything was gone,
All the oak trees cut in half,
All the strawberries eaten,
All the birds had flown away . . .
Because of the climate change!

Hannah Smith (10)
Iwade Community Primary School, Iwade

War Is . . .

War is hurt,
War is anger,
War is pain,
And war is danger.

War is fire,
War is thunder,
War is darkness,
And war is hunger.

War is bombs,
War is sirens,
War is air raids,
And seeking shelter.

Bring back love,
Bring back laughter,
Bring back joy,
And peace ever after.

Eleanor Young (9)
Iwade Community Primary School, Iwade

Rainforests

R ecycle now
A lways
I magine
N o
F orests
O r
R ain
E ver
S aving
T his
S pace again!

Lily Taylor (9)
Iwade Community Primary School, Iwade

Save The World

Save the world!
It needs your help
To know more about
Knowing how,
Look in books about
Storms!

It may tell you
How to improve
Your carbon footprint.
Tsunamis,
Hurricanes, tornadoes and floods,
Are battering
The world!

In London
People are living in boxes
In Ethiopia
They don't drink fresh water
In Indonesia
They have floods
In China
There was an earthquake.

How can we help?
Share resources?
Do our actions?
Change the climate?
How can we help
The victims?

Matthew Claydon (8)
John Mayne CE Primary School, Biddenden

The Bad Cold Life

I live in a box, a very small box.
No shelter, no house, no water and no food.
I starve to death all day long.
I eat any food,
Like carrots that have been on the dirty old ground,
A burger that has been in a disgusting bin all day long.

Every day I beg for money.
I am very happy . . . I get about a pound a day.
I wear rags and no shoes.
I wash in the river where people throw their rubbish,
But yet I don't have anything
Except me and my old, broken, stupid box!

My mother never wanted me and no one ever cared about me,
So I have to survive by myself.
I've never had any company
And my box is not going to last very much longer.

Rosie May Matthews (9)
John Mayne CE Primary School, Biddenden

Stop!

Stop killing endangered animals
Stop destroying their homes
Stop destroying their world
Stop taking their food
Stop drinking their water
Stop eating them
Stop people destroying the rainforest
Stop taking their world
Stop people killing their shade
Stop taking the forest
Stop taking their homes
Stop taking them!

Thomas Woulfe (9)
John Mayne CE Primary School, Biddenden

Iraq War

Hello, my name is Alice, all day long I hear bangs
And all I see are lots of gangs
But there are lots of men with guns
And no one ever sits down for buns

But all the time I see this
I mean, they have got to miss
All their family and friends
And they never have time to use pens

If I could do one thing
I know what it would be
I would stop the war
And everybody would dance with glee

And it is hard for me because I can't walk about
And it is harder when it is a drought
I can't go out and play
Because I am trapped inside all day

And here I am, all alone
With no one here at home
And no one here to play the games
And no one here to guess the names.

Alice Elizabeth Bevan (9)
John Mayne CE Primary School, Biddenden

Tramps On The Street

Tramps live in small boxes.
Tramps live on anything they can find that looks edible.
Tramps have smelly clothes.
Tramps wash in a river.
Tramps want more money.

William Sherriff (8)
John Mayne CE Primary School, Biddenden

Endangered Animals

I am a leopard running,
I see my prey,
I pounce.
Oh no! Not the dart!
Right in the ribs,
I have been taken!
I must fight back,
Quick *roar, scratch,*
Be quick and fight.
'You will never go free mutt.'
'I will claw on your cage and I will get out
I will!'
'You can do what you like, you will not be free.'
Yes! Here comes my dad, 'Quick Dad, quick.
Kill him, kill him, pounce on him
To set me free!'

We should not do this.

Lee Rossiter (9)
John Mayne CE Primary School, Biddenden

Why?

Why should people in Afghanistan suffer from war?
Why should people on the London streets live in boxes?
Why should trees be chopped down for boring homework?
Why should people in poorer places get killed from diseases?
And the rainforest animals are struggling to survive,
From their habitat being destroyed,
And litter is being dropped down on the streets.
People are dying in China from the earthquake,
And children in India are working and dying,
And people are getting killed in war.

Elliot John Steward (9)
John Mayne CE Primary School, Biddenden

The Helpless Homeless

I'm a poor old man living on the streets of London City.
No money, no friends, I eat from rubbish bins.
I sit in an old tattered box,
I have no roof only a newspaper as my cover.
I'm ill from eight diseases.
I've been injured in a street fight,
I've lost two fingers.
I'm freezing cold at night-time.
I've got rats in my box crawling everywhere.
I beg for money but the people just stare and laugh at me.
I'm scared of my own fellow people.
They treat me like a piece of rubbish on the streets.
Well, I guess that's what I really am, my life is wasted.
I'm a failure, no home, no family, no friends, no anything,
So please help me.
Soon I will *die!*

Tyla Trafford Reeves-Vane (9)
John Mayne CE Primary School, Biddenden

The War

Here I am, going to war in a tank
It is very hot in the tank
In the country
In Iraq
It is midnight
We are sleeping in the tank
We wake up, it is two o'clock in the morning
We get the guns ready and we start shooting
We wake people up
Then we get the rest of the team
They try to shoot people in a second
Millions of people die and we keep shooting and stealing
And man . . . people are dying in pain!
Then people start to shoot us.

Sammy Joe Beaney (9)
John Mayne CE Primary School, Biddenden

Endangered Animals

There are many countries and rainforests in the world.
But in hot rainforests, some creatures live,
Such as pandas and jaguars.
But still people go out and shoot them
And eat their meat on a roasted fire.

About two hundred pandas are left in the rainforests
And two hundred trees are left,
But these are being chopped down because of war.
Houses are being chopped down because of war.
Pandas live in trees
And we live in homes.
Pandas' homes being chopped down
Is like our houses being chopped down day after day.
So you are a small panda,
Next day you're lying dead!
So do not kill or chop down trees,
And definitely leave habitats and creatures alone.

Emily Rasmussen Arda (8)
John Mayne CE Primary School, Biddenden

No Home, No Life

Here I am in the street with no life, no home, only a box.
The only friend I have is a rat named Hobos.
My best item is a paperclip chain.
My day job is to beg,
Some people put in 1p,
Some people put in sticks, rocks and grass.
The only thing I get to eat is things out of the bin
And old hubby, bubblegum off walls.
What a life I have!
If only there were more houses.
Please improve my environment.

Connor Herbert
John Mayne CE Primary School, Biddenden

Endangered Animals

The Indian tiger is an endangered animal,
So we need to look after them.
The Snow tiger and the Indian tiger,
They are my favourite tigers.
I have four pictures.
I write about them.

Chimpanzee is a type of monkey,
It jumps from tree to tree.
The chimpanzees live in the rainforest.
Humans clear their tree habitat.

The African elephant is good for its tusks,
So it is shot by hunters
To sell the tusks.

We should not do this!
We need to look after our world.

Jack Thomas Beaney (9)
John Mayne CE Primary School, Biddenden

How Can I Go On?

I am living in a cardboard box
In London, I am helpless here.
I've got no friends, money, family, job,
Car or a home.
We could go out but they would say, 'You pay.'
But I would have no money to pay with
So I always say, 'No!'
I want to go to the aquarium.
My life is full of disappointments.

Sam Luke Hackney (9)
John Mayne CE Primary School, Biddenden

People, Poor And Rich

If people are poor and if people are rich,
They need to buy food and water.

Rich people can buy this or that, but poor people can't,
And they feel sad because they do not have enough money.
No money to go out and buy things like clothes for their families.
Rich people can do what they want for their families.
They get what they want for them, that's what the rich can do,
But poor people cannot do that as they have no money.

Priscilla Wagnone (9)
John Mayne CE Primary School, Biddenden

The Flood

In different countries there are floods.
Some people lose their homes.
But something like the ice melting is really bad.
Some people get trapped when there is a flood in London.
Some people don't live.
When the sea comes in . . . if it comes right in
It might cause a flood.
You might have one in the morning.

Laura Irons (9)
John Mayne CE Primary School, Biddenden

The Rainforest

Here I am in the rainforest watching the trees be cut down,
And I feel very sorry for the animals.
I feel really sad because
I can see lots of animals jumping from tree to tree.
Almost like diving,
They move so quickly.

Jodi Reid (9)
John Mayne CE Primary School, Biddenden

Endangered Lions

Lions should not be shot!

Lions are endangered species
If you keep on shooting them
Then when you have children
They won't be able to see them
And you will have to tell them about lions
And they will burst to see them.

And if we don't look after the lions
They will turn more and more evil.
Lions are ginger and brown.

Lions are getting shot for no reason.
You should stop shooting them
They haven't done anything to you.

Calvin Herbert
John Mayne CE Primary School, Biddenden

Why?

Why are poor people living in cardboard boxes?
Why are rich people living in big, fancy houses?
Why are people cutting down the rainforest?
Why can't people leave the rainforest as it is?
Why have we got money?
Why haven't poor people got money?
Why are kids in Iraq only seeing guns?
In Beijing there was an earthquake, why?
Why don't we put litter in the bin?
Why do we litter?

Why?

Let's be kind.

Daniel James Baker (9)
John Mayne CE Primary School, Biddenden

Will You Or Won't You?

Will you or won't you save our world?
Don't pollute the air,
Show you really care.
Don't drive in your car,
Unless you're going far.
Don't throw litter in the river,
It makes the fish quiver.
Don't destroy the trees,
They're filled with birds and bees.
Don't build more houses,
What'll happen to the foxes and mouses?
Don't make more factories,
We've got enough batteries.
Will you or won't you save our world?

Sophie Campion (10)
Knaphill School, Knaphill

An Unhappy World

It was so silent I heard . . .
Men chopping down trees and taking away oxygen.

It was so peaceful I saw . . .
Gas floating in our atmosphere and polluting the world.

It was still I felt . . .
Litter drop on the ground and being left there and never picked up.

It was so silent I could . . .
Hear God crying because his world is dying.

Josie Morschel (10)
Leigh Primary School, Leigh

Doing It For The World

If I had a bigger brain,
I'd work out a solution
To save the world and animals
From dangerous pollution.

If I could reverse one thing,
I'd replant all the trees,
To stop the world from arguing
And prevent World War III!

If I had a time machine,
I'd go back really far,
Back to train the dodos
To replace every car!

If I had a telescope,
I'd gaze up to the stars,
And send food up to aliens
Who might starve to death on Mars!

If I had a louder voice,
I'd let myself be seen,
By shouting out to all the world,
'Just make this place more green!'

Natalie Jobbins (10)
Leigh Primary School, Leigh

Keep The World Green

If I had wings,
I'd fly around the world,
Looking for things to tidy up
And set right.

If I had a wand,
I'd stop everyone from cutting down trees,
To have more food
And oxygen to breathe.

If I had a wand,
I'd make the people recycle everything and anywhere,
Whether they liked it or not.

If I had a wish,
I'd wish for lots more wishes,
So I could wish the world a better place to live in.

If I had a cloud,
I'd make it rain all day,
So all the plants and trees could grow
And everyone could play.

Louise Large (10)
Leigh Primary School, Leigh

The Big Green Machine

It was so silent . . .
I could hear all the poor
crying out for help.

It was so peaceful . . .
I could hear the rustle of litter
being dropped on the ground.

It was so still . . .
I could hear the rumble of war
and the dying falling on the ground
crying for help.

It was so calm . . .
I could feel the seas
being drained of their water.

It was so silent . . .
I could hear all the trees groaning
as they were being chopped down
by chainsaws and axes.

Nicholas Connell (9)
Leigh Primary School, Leigh

A Dying World

It was so silent . . .
I heard the ozone layer
Fading away.

It was so peaceful . . .
I heard the homeless people
Wasting away.

It was so still . . .
I saw the cars on the street
Burning petrol all day.

It was so silent . . .
I heard the cry of the tiger
Dying in pain.

It was so still . . .
I felt the snow melt to water
Because of climate change.

It was so calm . . .
I sensed the world
Crying for help . . .

It's all down to us!

Charlotte Doherty (10)
Leigh Primary School, Leigh

Recycling

R ubbish every day.
E gg boxes sitting on a shelf.
C ardboard, always recycle it.
Y oghurt pots, useful for stuff.
C at food tins.
L orries taking the recycling material.
I ndian takeaway boxes.
N oodle pots.
G reen carrier bags.

Rhiannon Pond (8)
Luton Junior School, Chatham

Recycling Litter Poem

Used-up papers, don't throw them away
They can be used for another day
Plastic, metal, paper too
Recycling is what you should do
Don't go binning all those toys
Give them to other girls and boys
Use those carrier bags twice
Reusing things is nice
Sort out your glass, paper and tin
Then take them to the recycling bin.

Reisa McFarlane (8)
Luton Junior School, Chatham

Saving The Planet

Please put rubbish in the bin.
It will help us.
Throw only these things in the bin,
Like garden waste and glass,
Plastic bottles and clothes.
Do you want to save the planet?
Well, now is your chance.

Zuzana Kucerkova (8)
Luton Junior School, Chatham

Goodbye Black Bags

B lue is great, black is horrible
L et black bags go away
U nkind black bag, let blue bags take your place
E arth is being polluted.

Joe MacKay (9)
Luton Junior School, Chatham

Recycle Please!

Think *blue* not black!
Take out your blue recycling bin or your recycling sack!
Recycling saves men digging underground,
Or controlling bulldozers to throw all the rubbish down.
It's ruining our Earth and ground!
Come on, take out your recycling bin and your recycling sack!
Trust me, I know we can do better than that!
Just remember about all the poor families and people
                                    in other countries.
Poor them, they don't have any money.
Remember we can still help every single one,
Just by recycling, don't be lazy, come!
Let's not create any more disasters!
If we work together this entire world will be saved!
No more poor people craving! I hate to see them crave!
Just one simple thing (recycling) and everyone will be
                                    happy and healthy.
Everyone will take you as a hero! You won't be a number zero!
Please recycle, make the world a fascinating place!
Every single person will have a smile on his or her face!
Please recycle! Thank you.

Rasha Vadamootoo (9)
Luton Junior School, Chatham

Recycling

R is for rubbish, we produce more each day.
E is for extinction, animals can become extinct.
C is for clutter, don't bin it, recycle it.
Y is for yoghurt pots, we can reuse them.
C is for children teaching parents to recycle.
L is for the litter we bin.
I is for I see a future where people recycle.
N is for nasty smells when we bin stuff.
G is for garden waste we recycle.

Jazmine Higgins (8)
Luton Junior School, Chatham

Save Our Planet

Recycling is fun!
My mum has got a ton!
Recycling is good
As it should be.
We need to save the Earth.
Today an animal lies worrying about extinction.
Help the planet!
It needs help, start today.
Farewell normal day.
You can sing without a CD player.
You can leave one light on when watching the big game.
Besides you're saving money.
Think about the polar bears in large caves.
No more BBC animal programmes.
Think of the scientists - no animals to study.
Recycle now, before it is too late!

Cheyenne Beaney (9)
Luton Junior School, Chatham

Think Of The Future

Papers with yesterday's news
Thrown away without a clue.
Tins and cans are better saved
If we do, new things can be made.

Recycle and new things can be made,
A plane, a car or a new knife blade.
Forests full of trees and wood,
Would make new furniture if it could.

Clothing that no longer fits,
Can go to countries that will use it.

We must really stop and think.
As the world is now on the brink,
Of becoming a dumping ground
For all the stuff we no longer want around.

Olivia Grist (8)
Luton Junior School, Chatham

I Am The Earth

I am the Earth, a beautiful place
Where birds and sparrows sing
I am the Earth, a beautiful place
Where plants grow thick and thin

The animals live in harmony
The air is fresh and clean
I am the Earth, a beautiful place
Where every living thing has been.

Then Man came and broke me down
He cut my trees for wood
He killed the animals for their fur
I wondered how he could.

The factories were choking me
The air was getting warm
But all I could do was watch and weep
Because Man was killing his own.

Children of the world, come and save me
My future is in your hands
Stop these men from destroying me
And give me back my lands.

Don't use plastic, use paper or glass
Don't drive, maybe cycle to school
Be kind to your neighbour, whatever his colour
For he is your brother too.

Give back to the soil what you have taken from it
Grow lots of plants and trees
I am the Earth, a beautiful place,
Let's keep it that way, *please!*

Satvik Subramaniam (9)
St John's Beaumont School, Old Windsor

Environment

Keep the environment green and clean.
We want it to last beyond our teens
get out of your cars and use your feet
we need to stop producing heat.

Turn down your boilers
use the sun
those electric sources
don't need to run and run.

Use less water
don't have a bath
have a shower with a cap
use rain for the garden
not from the tap.

Recycle your rubbish
it's good and true
separate bins and bags
the environment needs *you!*

Josh Rogers (9)
St John's Beaumont School, Old Windsor

The Wasted Environment

Our environment is wasting away
And we don't have anything to say
We'll have to try to conserve this wonderful planet
But people are not doing their part
But they are not smart
We have to do our part to conserve
The world's heart, we know that we
Have people in our rainforests trying to help,
We have to play our vital part
Let's be very smart, let's do our part today.

Nikhil Sharma (11)
St John's Beaumont School, Old Windsor

Climate Changes

Don't destroy our forests
as the trees keep air clean,
they neutralise carbon dioxide
which helps the fish in our streams.
Instead of using a car, just use a bicycle,
when you've finished with your clothes,
don't dump them, just recycle,
when we use electricity, we burn energy.
Be good to the Earth
and it'll be good to you!

Christian Taee (9)
St John's Beaumont School, Old Windsor

Global Warming

Brilliant beaches
Wonderful waterfalls
Fantastic forests
Massive mountains

Ice melting
Rivers flooding
Storms breaking
Earth quaking

Big warning
Global warming!

James Mainwaring (8)
St John's Beaumont School, Old Windsor

The Earth

E nvironment, the place we live in
A pple, a fruit that we eat
R ecycle plastic and card
T hen the factories that pollute
H elp to look after the Earth.

Robert Cook (11)
St John's Beaumont School, Old Windsor

What's Happening To Our World?

What's happening to our world,
The one we love so dear?
They are chopping down the woodlands
Causing animals so much fear.

What's happening to our world?
The seas men over-fish,
They are greedy and they are selfish,
Shipping fish off to different lands
To put on people's dish.

What's happening to our world?
Men killing one another,
They think of no one but themselves
Not even their own brother.

So let's not kill our world
And definitely not one another!

Jack Spink (9)
St John's Beaumont School, Old Windsor

Work As A Team To Help The World

The world needs help not to throw rubbish on the ground.

I had a dream last night
The world was a better place for better people.
The sea was clean like a blue dream.
The world was safe like a better place.
Forests were green and clean like a green dream.
Mountains were white and light.
People were happy and playful
The world was a happy, living place.

Charles Boileve (9)
St John's Beaumont School, Old Windsor

The World Is Such A Beautiful Place

The world was such a beautiful place,
but the beauty has left without a trace.
The trees were dying and the grass was crying
with no one for relying . . .

The world is such a beautiful place,
the world is so full of grace.
Now the trees gleam, while the grass is green
and the birds fly free.

The world could be an even more beautiful place,
there could be more open space.
The trees could be living.
The grass could be singing.

The world will never ask for something back
but it will keep on giving.

Thomas Martins da Silva (9)
St John's Beaumont School, Old Windsor

All Our Fault

An animals so alone and lonely
Struggling in a caged world,
Is a poor, ugly antelope,
People laughing as the antelope cries,
To try and ignore us.

This has all happened
Because of all the chopping and hunting
We did all this, so
To free wildlife,
Please stop doing all this.

The natural reserves are burning away
You will then have nothing to say.

Ryan Shum ((10)
St John's Beaumont School, Old Windsor

Boom!

The big green poetry machine,
helps turn the world green,
with plant poetry,
and songs about a honeybee.

We must recycle and cycle,
instead of going in cars,
if we don't want the Earth,
to be as red as Mars.

We must not refuse to reuse
our waste in our haste,
to make this world
a better place.

If we don't do something soon,
our world will go *boom!*

Harry Chan (9)
St John's Beaumont School, Old Windsor

We Can Save The World!

Global warming can destroy the Earth.
We must fight greenhouse gases.
It is the only way to save the masses.
It is easy, so why do we find it so hard
To stop destroying the planet?

Do your bit for the environment
And turn off lights and save electricity.
Don't chop down trees, leave them,
It is better for the environment.

Turn off taps and save water,
Hip hip hooray!
Start today and save the world!

Oliver Smith (9)
St John's Beaumont School, Old Windsor

The Future

The flowers are red, the sky is blue,
what will happen to me and you?
The world is a mess like my desk,
we have to tidy up for the best.
People beware, the cutting of trees
can lead to drought, famine and disease.
Recycle and reuse, and do not abuse.
Plastic bags we must refuse.
Water we must not waste
for the sake of the human race!
Global warming is bad,
it makes me feel very sad.
We must try and make the world live in peace,
poverty and conflict must cease.
The flowers are red, the sky is blue,
the future is now up to you!

Ian Yorke (9)
St John's Beaumont School, Old Windsor

Save The World

The sun came out, it was shining,
The sky was bubbly blue,
White clouds all around,
I woke up and looked out,
I said, *'Wow!'*
But suddenly it all changed,
The sky was grey,
There were loads of clouds,
You could not see the sun,
It was dark and awful,
The flowers were dying,
Take all the pollution out of the world,
Save the world from dying!

Alessandro Tenconi (9)
St John's Beaumont School, Old Windsor

Save The Planet

Danger, danger everywhere
Global warming we all should care
Come on everybody save the trees
Before you know it we'll have no air to breathe
Pollution means the world is not clean
Leave your car behind if you are so keen
Stop hunting the animals that are rare
You don't need a tortoise frame or a rug from a grizzly bear
Everybody can help save the planet, even you
Everybody can contribute and you will feel happy *too!*

Max Cunningham (9)
St John's Beaumont School, Old Windsor

Recycling

R ubbish is growing
E missions are flowing
C arbon is burning
Y es, we need to start learning
C ardboard, cartons, plastic and tins
L andfill is what we put in our bins.
I f the planet is to be saved
N ow the way must be paved . . .
G reen waste is needed for another day.

Henry Gray (9)
St John's Beaumont School, Old Windsor

The Ocean

The sea is full of drift,
As selfish people come along,
And throw their litter in the sea!
But they kill the fish, sharks and jellyfish too!
And so many other sea animals.

Marcus Thevarajan (8)
St John's CE School, Middlesex

Water, Litter And Recycle

Turn the water off so you don't waste it.
Run around in the street instead of using cars.
Recycle every day so that you can reuse it.
Don't put candy on the ground because it will get smelly,
So eat the candy because it belongs in your belly.
Look at the sea, look at the waves, it is so peaceful.
But I see someone putting rubbish in the sea and that's bad,
So put the rubbish in the bin instead, because that's a good thing.
Do not smoke, it is so bad that you can make someone ill.
So stop smoking and you will be fine.
Saving the environment is a good thing,
Because you are saving the world.
Also you are saving the animals.
Thank you for saving the Earth.

Cherise Jarrett (8)
St John's CE School, Middlesex

Save My Sea!

I am a fish, I always listen to the waves near caves,
I always hear the boats near the moats.
I have a sis but my life is not bliss,
Because people keep throwing rubbish into the sea,
So bliss is not the life for me!

Alana Gaglio (8)
St John's CE School, Middlesex

Food For Animals - Song

Animals eat juicy old leaves,
Young little animals eat young leaves,
Some pandas like to eat bamboo sticks,
Then they change their minds and eat leaves.
Animals eat all different kinds of leaves.

Michelle Gowrialnathan (7)
St John's CE School, Middlesex

Flowers

We love to keep the world so clean.
We have some secrets we would like to share
So listen to what we say . . .

Sunflowers are so big and tall
with lots of seeds for you to make oil and eat.
Daisies are so small and cute you can make daisy chains
but not too many otherwise we will all die.
Roses are so posh and red with a long green stem
with prickles and thorns, try not to poke your finger!
Lavender is a long purple flower with a lovely scent
you can only describe as Heaven!

Maximilian Mollenhauer-Starkl (8)
St John's CE School, Middlesex

The Sea Is Blue

The sea is blue, but now turning brown
Let's help make it blue again.
The sparkle of the sun makes the sea glimmer.
The sealife that dies doesn't get to say goodbye.
The gentle flyers silently swoop across the bright blue sky.
When the sun shines it does not sparkle, no, it doesn't shine.
Come on people, let's go and save the Earth!

Nathan Ferguson (8)
St John's CE School, Middlesex

What Lovely Sea

The sea is such a lovely place
but only if you don't chuck your stinky, smelly litter in,
Then people can swim in the sea,
And if you are those people that chuck litter in,
Don't, because *you're killing the fish.*
Stop polluting the sea.

Darryl Giffts-Walker (7)
St John's CE School, Middlesex

In The Sea

I love the sea it is beautiful.
It is sparkling and shiny but there is only one problem,
Nobody takes care of it,
So it gets attacked,
So you should take care of the sea.
So you must take of the sea
So we can see the blue of it.

Rosh Emmanuel (8)
St John's CE School, Middlesex

The Disaster

The sea is so blue it sparkles like stars,
But ships are a threat to the animals.
Nets can hurt dolphins too.
Fishermen catch fish and eat them.
If you throw plastic bags in the sea
You can kill animals.

Joseph Brady (8)
St John's CE School, Middlesex

Ocean Trouble

The ocean likes to be pretty, sparkly, wavy too.
Down in the deep ocean you can see dolphins, fish, starfish too.
The animals like to swim in the pretty water,
But sometimes people throw garbage in the ocean, cans,
                                        chocolate wrappers too
But worst of all, boats go past, *beep, beep,* and spread pollution.

Blyth McPherson (8)
St John's CE School, Middlesex

Look After Me!

I am the sea
Look after me.

My fish are dying
Oils are polluting.

I am the beautiful sea,
But they are polluting me.

Look after me!

Joelle Phua (8)
St John's CE School, Middlesex

Destroying The World!

Habitat fading away
Animals fading away
Plants fading away

Invisible killer
Silence increasing
Thunder's hitting
Ice melting
Water rising
Lips peeling.

Hanna Touhami (10)
Sacred Heart Primary School, Battersea

Wasting Water

There once was a reporter
Who wanted to live in Malta.
But the country was dry,
So he couldn't get by
Because his colleagues were used too much more water.

Freddy Eytle (10)
Sacred Heart Primary School, Battersea

Worries

A nimal-eater
B lack-hole
C old-treatment
D eath-starter
E arth-exterminator
F lood-beginning
G reat-heat
H uman-torture
I ce-melter
J ustice-unfair
K angaroo-killer
L ove-destroyer
M any-scares
N ot-fair
O h-pain
P eople-poisoner
Q uick-death
R acing-time bomb
S ad-ending
T icking-bomb
U nbearable-suspense
V ulture-attack
W hat's happening?
X -tra-distress
Y -us?
Z oo-terror.

Courtney Greaves (10)
Sacred Heart Primary School, Battersea

The Poem About Electricity

There once was a girl, Felicity,
Who loved to waste electricity.
The light had a spark,
Then the house went dark
And then she moved out of the city.

Esther Nkwusi (10)
Sacred Heart Primary School, Battersea

My Kennings

Storm-starter
Poverty-happening
Flood-increasing
Soil-drier
Sweat-bringer
Lips-cracking
Chaos-arriving
World-ender
Heat-expander
Cancer-increaser
Sun-shining
Ice-melter
Drought-finisher
Chaos has arrived.

Dominic James McCoy (10)
Sacred Heart Primary School, Battersea

Our Planet's Death!

The heat-bringer
A life-taker
A lake-goes
The-sea-will-rise
Our-lungs-choke
For-the-killer
Stalks-our-ground.

Birds-don't-fly
People-cry
Whales-go-dry
Life is gone.

Thomas Maton (10)
Sacred Heart Primary School, Battersea

Global Warming

Good causer
Ice melter
Cancer producer
Life threatener
Animal rotter
Planet burner
River trasher
Invisible issue
Dead hazardous
Chaotic destruction.

Marco Minoletti (10)
Sacred Heart Primary School, Battersea

Rubbish

Rubbish
Smelly, ugly,
Wasting, filling, steaming.
It's filling up our street.
Nasty!

Thomas Smith (9)
Sacred Heart Primary School, Battersea

Is The World Over?

Is the world over as we know it . . . ?
Global warming!
Global warming!
Warning of the heat
Ice is melting
The sun is coming
Earth refuses to die.

Louis Wright (10)
Sacred Heart Primary School, Battersea

Global Warming

Humid hell
Flood causer
Animal killer
Earth radiator
Tongue sweller
World slayer
Oxygen decreaser
Animal agony
Cancer creator
Crop killer.

World ender!

Rachelle Anera Ogello (9)
Sacred Heart Primary School, Battersea

Untitled

Air poisoner
Animal killer
Litter walker
Death stalker
Life eater
Street beater
Human slayer
World annihilator.

Nicole Agyekurn (9)
Sacred Heart Primary School, Battersea

Stage Lights

There once was a man called Yoarmer
Who always was a performer,
He went on stage
With all his rage
And became the *global warmer!*

Ethan Laurent (10)
Sacred Heart Primary School, Battersea

Power

There once was a girl who loved flowers
She lived in a great big tower
She kept the lights on
The place always shone
She always loved when she had a shower for an hour.

Amani Clarke (9)
Sacred Heart Primary School, Battersea

Our Dying World

Dying
Sad, mad,
Drifting, falling, slipping,
Slipping quickly out of mind,
Dead!

Araba Mercer Banson (10)
Sacred Heart Primary School, Battersea

Water

Water
Crystal clear blue
Changing, drifting, loitering,
Polluted by our awful waste!
H_2O!

Radhika Nagar (10)
Sacred Heart Primary School, Battersea

Rubbish

Ugly, smelly,
Filthy, smelly, homely,
It's hurting the amazing world,
Hateful!

Oliwia Jaruzel (10)
Sacred Heart Primary School, Battersea

Nasty Stuff

Nasty stuff.
Rubbish!
Smelly, dirty.
Filling, wasting, steaming.
Destroying our lovely land.
Junk!

Victor Kopp (10)
Sacred Heart Primary School, Battersea

Global Warming

Poverty-bringer
Environmental-murderer
Glacier-melter
Generation-disappointer
Preventing-life
Unseen-terror.

Charles Hill (10)
Sacred Heart Primary School, Battersea

Global Warming

There was a thing called global warming
Which only came up in the morning
It heated like the sun
That burst someone's bum
And only found out whilst yawning!

Steven Da Silva (10)
Sacred Heart Primary School, Battersea

Water

There once was the king's daughter
Who wanted to be a reporter.
She said to the queen,
'Why are you so mean?'
So she stopped wasting water.

Reiss Ormonde Cunningham (10)
Sacred Heart Primary School, Battersea

The Tiger

Prowling and growling through the night,
On the riverbank in the moonlight,
Flames in the last few tigers' eyes,
One who looks at the starry skies.

'Save us! Save us!' calls a shout,
Coming from the river, splashing about,
Only the ones who can hear their cries,
Can see the flames in the tigers' eyes.

Angharad Eburne (10)
The Grey House School, Hartley Wintney

Endangered Animals

So many animals are endangered
The Red List is a bit long to say
We have to stop using pesticides
Or we will lose insects as well
And if we lose insects everything will die.
So this is my final warning
Take care!

Reuben Chasey (9)
The Grey House School, Hartley Wintney

The Drums Of War

Our world is full of hate,
People making a bad mistake.
Going to war is bad,
Because of it people are very sad.

People starving, stomachs weak,
Not much food around to eat.
Everywhere, grey and murky,
Everyone a little jerky.

Bang, bang! A gun has shot,
Dropping bombs onto a lot.
People screaming for their mums,
But no one to hear them because of the drums.

The war has come to an end now,
People dead on the floor, *wow.*
'How many dead, Sir?'
'10,000,' said Sir Curr.

All those men and women lying on the floor,
Just because of a stupid old war!

Grace Gratwick (11)
The Grey House School, Hartley Wintney

Pollution

P eople must learn to stop polluting
O ver half the world guilty
L iving creatures in danger
L iving a 'green' life can make them safe
U ndo this bad deed
T his is something you can do to make a change
I ndividuals changing a piece of our planet
O thers follow, a great change
N ow this is all you have to remember . . .

Stop the pollution!

Saskia Chandler (11)
The Grey House School, Hartley Wintney

The Tiger

Through the long grass
The tiger sees a deer pass
So he creeps
Step by step.

He springs into the air
And roars, *'Beware!'*
With the deer's eaten skin
This means that the tiger wins.

With the tiger's mighty fear
The other tigers all cheer
It's the end of the day
And the tiger goes away.

Rishi Shah (10)
The Grey House School, Hartley Wintney

Save The World!

Save the world while you can
Stop leaving lights on
Turn taps off.
Don't throw carrier bags overboard
Turtles eat them and die.
They sink
Slowly
Down to the bottom of the sea.
Animals are suffering
They shouldn't suffer!
So, *stop* and think
Save the world!

Verity Jackson (9)
The Grey House School, Hartley Wintney

Recycling

Recycle our world!
Recycle glass bottles
Recycle plastic bags
Recycle cardboard
Recycle newspaper and paper
Recycle clothes

Recycling
  Is
  Good!

Henry Cummings (9)
The Grey House School, Hartley Wintney

The Tiger

The tiger glows like a lamp
Its eyes are like stars
It runs like a shooting star
Its coat is like a sunset

The tiger sleeps like a baby
It stalks its prey like a child playing
Its teeth are like diamonds
It walks as elegantly as a cat.

Natasha Lee (10)
The Grey House School, Hartley Wintney

My Name

I have a name, I'm called, 'Help I'm Dying'!
I have a name, I'm called, 'Help, There's Too Much Heat'!
I have a name, I'm called, 'My Icebergs Are Melting'.
I have a name, I'm called 'Earth'!

Joseph Allen (9)
The Grey House School, Hartley Wintney

What Lies Beneath Sight

In our world the trees never forget and will always remember,
As I wander through the trees,
Images flash in my mind of long-forgotten lives,
Ones that were evil,
Ones that were kind,
Ones that were ended by the slow-falling knife.
Lives of murderers,
Lives of children,
Lives of the dead,
The ground covered in light as well as darkness,
The bleakness of many crowds the floor,
In this world, the lives of men have been lost
To fate or the crazed maniac of death.
The footprints,
The deathly cold air,
The blackness.
In the branches, joy is growing,
But also the wickedness of people haunts the trees.
The trees hold all of this, so why end their lives?
What one man dreams is another man's destiny.

Aaron Ueckermann (11)
The Grey House School, Hartley Wintney

Tiger Tales!

Down in the jungle,
The beautiful jungle,
The tiger stalks its prey!

Its colours are like the sunset, glowing in the night.
Its teeth shine and are as sharp as daggers
And its eyes glow like fire.

Hannah Byrne (10)
The Grey House School, Hartley Wintney

Global Warming On Four Wheels

Notice:

There is a criminal who is planning to murder Earth,
with his deadliest weapon, global warming.
Already the dodo, lowland gorilla and polar bear
have been killed or are suffering from his other weapon, hunting.
He moves around on four wheels,
Is about twelve feet long and five feet high,
His name is Car.
If you see him, please phone

Thank you,
Royal Nature
Police Industry.

Robert Cootes (9)
The Grey House School, Hartley Wintney

Save The World

S top polluting rivers.
A nimals, like birds are in danger because people cut down trees.
V ery much of the world needs to recycle.
E verybody should drink lots of water.

T he world can be a better place.
H elp the world to be more environmentally friendly.
E nd cutting down trees.

W orldwide, people need to recycle,
O r the planet will be more damaged.
R ubbish shouldn't be thrown on the floor.
L ook to see what you can do to help.
D o your part to help the environment.

James Myland (8)
The Grey House School, Hartley Wintney

The Flame

In the midst of the jungle the tiger roars,
The creature is a flame of orange and black.
A flame that only bullets can penetrate.
His roar fills the sky, the Earth and sea,
But mankind blocks it out.

All around the grassland,
Animals run and clear.
The flame is approaching,
The flame that water can't put out.

As most bow down and others scatter,
He prowls around the trees.
The flame is here! Majestic and strong,
The owner of the jungle.

The creatures of the Earth cheer and whoop,
The stars reach down to touch him.
With one last roar he slinks into the trees,
The flame has gone, the beautiful flame . . .
The flame that we put out.

Holly Smith (10)
The Grey House School, Hartley Wintney

Stalking Tiger

Coat burning bright orange, like a fire.
Eyes like golden trophies.
Teeth like knives as long as fingers,
Claws sharp as needles, extending.

Much longer than a man is tall,
But blending in, so that grass and animal become a blur.
Totally focused, pointing like a dagger towards its prey.
Ready for the deadly strike.

Jack Shemwell (10)
The Grey House School, Hartley Wintney

The Tiger

The creature, the beast, the thing,
Prowling as grace carries by.
The eyes of death, the stripes of glory,
No creature compares to thee.
The Maker of the lamb
Made it to live the worthiest of lives,
He looks among the animals, to make them fear.

The creature, the beast, the thing,
He lives in Heaven,
But the deathly scowl of Hell is within him.
Ten thousand lives are nothing, when he stalks his prey.
With elegance and death, when he pounces in an instant.
Nothing is faster when, at night, to claim a life,
The dark cannot stop the slaughter.
The creature, the beast, the tiger.

Barnaby Ridley (9)
The Grey House School, Hartley Wintney

Tiger

At night the prowling tiger, he stalks his prey, quiet and slow,
Closer and closer he will go,
Hidden in the long grass, crouching low,
Waiting to deliver his fatal blow.

Stretching out those tiger claws,
He bites his kill with his deadly jaws,
Now with his stomach full, he lies and snores,
Waiting for dawn while licking his paws.

Rory Bertuzzi-Glover (10)
The Grey House School, Hartley Wintney

Plastic Bags

'Plastic bags I don't like,' said a turtle one day.
'I wish they weren't invented on the Earth, OK?
We are being killed so help us if you can.
Don't buy plastic bags.
It will help us, it will save us!'

Anoushka Chandler (9)
The Grey House School, Hartley Wintney

War

War goes on around the world.
Though we try to stop the wars
They just get worse and worse.
But if we work together,
We have a better chance to stop the wars.
If we stop the wars we will be heroes.
War,
It makes the soldiers want more,
It makes them want to kill more and more.
So please help to stop the wars!

Ross Hayden (10)
The Hill Primary School, Caversham

Extinction

Why do we have extinction?
All those animals going, don't you miss them?
Don't you miss the dodo birds?
The brown feathers flying in the sky.
You know, in ten years time, we might not have any polar bears.
So think about all those animals that are gone.
Think about who is going!

Amy Lewis (11)
The Hill Primary School, Caversham

War

All day soldiers fall,
Crashed and thundered like a crumbling wall,
Some kill all day,
Others die and fade away,
Most fighting and brave,
Without knowing families are in graves,
Is war right
Or should they carry on the fight?
Some will return alive,
Others will dive.
It will never stop
Unless we prevent this strop,
It can't be ignored,
Or else it will get stored.
So let's work together and get rid of all the armour,
So we can work towards harmony.

Jonathon Venner (11)
The Hill Primary School, Caversham

Litter, Litter Everywhere!

Clatter, bang, crunch, squelch
I wade through this putrid swamp.

Coke cans, sweet wrappers, plastic bags,
They're all in the mix somewhere.

'Oi! Watch it!' I say,
'That takeaway hit me on the head!'

'Hey! Mind out!' I remark,
'That bottle landed in my lunch!'

Litter, litter everywhere!

Alex Hamilton (11)
The Hill Primary School, Caversham

Disease, Litter

D ying people
I need medication
S traight away
E veryone lying in their graves
A deadly disease
S ad parents crying over the dead children
E ventually everyone is dead.

L eftover rubbish
I put mine in the bin
T hough some people drop it on the floor
T hose people just don't care about the
E nvironment at all
R ubbish belongs in the bin!

Andrew McDonald (11)
The Hill Primary School, Caversham

The Lake

I, the lake, stream contentedly,
I, the mighty lake, gush powerfully,
I, the lake, am pure, protected, unharmed,

I, the lake, am seen by the sunlight glitter,
I, the bewitching lake, am shining like the moonlight,
I, the lake, am calm, respected, untouched,
I, the lake, three years later, nothing's the same,
I, the frail lake, unable to move,
I, the lake, am harmed, endangered, fouled,

I, the lake, am poisoned till I'm unseen,
I, the lake, am polluted,
Polluted till everything is gone.

Nicole Lai (11)
The Hill Primary School, Caversham

Little African Child, Don't You Cry

Little African child, don't you cry
Nothing can be done
To save your future from fate
This battle cannot be won.

Little African child, don't you cry
All you can do is live your life
Make it fun and make it happy
With very little strife.

Little African child, don't you cry
People really do care
About your life and your health
There are worse diseases out there.

Beri Wasylciw (11)
The Hill Primary School, Caversham

Panicking Pollution

Our monster cars,
Our flashing lights,
Our greenhouse gases,
Contribute to the world's disease.

The disease that . . .
Makes the cold, cold Arctic ice melt,
Makes the fragile ozone layer break,
Makes the emerald die.

We can stop the suffering,
We will make the unclean air
Fresh and free,
Causing merriment and cheer, not sorrow.

Zoe Wright (11)
The Hill Primary School, Caversham

War Is Horror

W ar
A ction
R age

I nvasion
S trife

H ostile
O peration
R esistance
R aging
O utrage
R ubble.

Dan Smith (11)
The Hill Primary School, Caversham

Racism

R aged
A ngry
C ruel
I mpure
S cared
M ean.

Lewis Jenkins (10)
The Hill Primary School, Caversham

Racism

R acism
A ngry people
C annot call people names
I t's a disgrace
S ad
M ean.

Daniel Tanner (11)
The Hill Primary School, Caversham

Go Green!

Don't drive your car,
Use your bike,
Or you could go for a hike.
It will keep you fit,
For a bit.
So carry on,
Quick, quick, quick.

Littering is bad,
It makes people sad.
There are bins,
So do not sin,
Carry on,
Quick, quick, quick.

Please go green,
Become clean.
So carry on,
Quick, quick, quick.

Sarah Eley (11)
The Hill Primary School, Caversham

War

War, war,
Horrible war,
Why can't we stop it?
Who knows?

War, war,
Disgusting war,
Why can't we stop it?
No one knows.

War, war,
It's really horrid,
I don't like it,
No one likes it.

Jack Gordon (10)
The Hill Primary School, Caversham

Don't Be Mean, Go Green!

Listen everyone,
I've got something to say.
You've been horrible, destroying your world.
Do you think that's OK?

Think about all the people who have
Suffered more than you.
Don't forget the plants and animals
Who got involved too.
Go green, go green!

You've been polluting the planet,
Chopping down trees,
Fighting at war, giving people disease.
Go green, go green!

Try to remember to turn the tap off,
Or not using smoke from cars to destroy crops.
Don't go to war to make people lame,
In the end you'll be to blame.

Go green, go green!
Who started this? You!
Who's making it continue? You!
Who's going to stop it? You!

Hannah Wetten
The Hill Primary School, Caversham

Nature Is Gone - Haiku

All the army men
Try to prove them different,
And nature is gone.

Jessica Bradbury (11)
The Hill Primary School, Caversham

The World Can Be Bad

It all started with a row
It ended a big fight
A war is on
The screams and shouts
Of people in the streets

Listening for the deadly cannon
Waiting in their sleep
Hoping it will be all right
But not necessarily for some
The homeless out all alone
Frightened like a mouse
Homeless, scared and fearful of what might come

Soldiers prowling down the roads
Some crying out in pain
Waiting for help to come
But most lying still
The child looks on in pain but not daring to walk away

We have to help
We can't just leave them there
They need love and care
For a good childhood

Don't just stare
Help the homeless, who are in despair!

Becky Beech (11)
The Hill Primary School, Caversham

No More - Haiku

Great tree fall to ground
Forest noise silenced by pain
Monkey, home no more.

Chiara Sexton (10)
The Hill Primary School, Caversham

Go Green

Reuse your plastic bags
And recycle your old mags,
Make something with bits of old card
And it's really not that hard.

Go green, go green, go green, green, green.

Don't leave on your hose
When you go for a little doze.
Don't go in the bath for an hour,
Instead have a five minute shower.

Go green, go green, go green, green, green.

Don't use your car
Or you'll get left with a pollution scar.
Don't drop your litter
Or the world will go bitter.

Go green, go green, go green, green, green.

Turn off your light
Because the sun is very bright.
Turn off your telly
Or your brain will turn to jelly.

Go green, go green, go green, green, green.

Daisy Smith (10)
The Hill Primary School, Caversham

Homelessness

All these people living on the street
While we sit in our houses all shiny and neat,
Holding out a hat asking for money
And yet some people think it's funny.
What would you say if you felt what it was like?
No freshly made bed or brand new bike.
But if we all tried to help them and donated an old DVD
They could all sit down and have some warm tea.

Djuna Mount (10)
The Hill Primary School, Caversham

Go Green!

Go green, go green,
Turn off the light,
When it's bright,
Don't waste water,
Or life will be shorter.

Go green, go green,
Don't drive your car,
Bikes take you just as far,
Turn off the heating when it's really hot,
How much cheaper will it be? Definitely a lot!

Go green, go green,
Recycle your card,
It's really not hard,
Don't use your hose,
To water your rose.

Go green, go green,
Don't be mean,
Go green!

Kayleigh Phillipps (11)
The Hill Primary School, Caversham

War

War, war not worth it anymore,
Bombs landing in front of doors.
War, war not worth it anymore.
No more war will be wonderful for all.
War, war no more.
It is long forgotten now and we move on!
People go to war to fight for their country.
Some people get hurt and die,
Some wars still go on,
Why, why, why?
There should be no more war *anymore!*

Cally Beale-Fletcher (11)
The Hill Primary School, Caversham

Helping The Animals

In this world animals are being tortured
Doing tricks for treats
Never allowed out
Jumping through fire hoops
Never allowed out.

People making a living
Hurting animals
Never allowed out
Lions and tigers kept in captivity
Never allowed out.

We have to let the animals escape
From our world into their paradise.

Daniella Luff (11)
The Hill Primary School, Caversham

War All The Time

The guns go bang, all day to night,
For the soldiers it is a big fright,
Some shoot during the day,
While the rest hide away,
War cannot be so right.

If you think war is so bad,
Look deep inside and you'll be quite glad,
Soldiers fight for you
Through wind, sun and rain,
They always fight with all they have.

Stephen Barr (11)
The Hill Primary School, Caversham

Laws Of Wars

Why war?
Why war?
Why hurt?
Why fight?
Why kill?
Why do people do these terrible things?
Who cares who is right or wrong?
Some people are killed in wars.
So why do we do these painful things?
Why war?
Why war?
Why war? Why war?

Morgan Lucie Field (10)
The Hill Primary School, Caversham

War Is Death

W orthless bashing and killing
A nd countries are getting destroyed
R are animals dying

I t will make us extinct
S ome men still live

D eath is sudden
E very man will die
A death, lots of men die
T he human race will die
H aving death is vile.

Sam Jones (11)
The Hill Primary School, Caversham

The Plague

Plague spreads,
Horrible and vicious,
It can snatch lives,
Forgives no one.
Some of the time it isn't bad,
Just like a cold,
But when it gets serious,
Results are delirious.
When you catch the plague
You need to take medicine,
A thick dreadful liquid,
Or a scary-looking pill.
You're in bed all day,
Sometimes in hospital,
Nothing to do,
You feel useless.
I am like a hunter
Closing in on a deer,
Getting ready to strike
On its unlucky prey.
I will terrorise everyone,
Anything in my way,
Attack bodies,
Take out cells.

Harry Baxter (11)
The Hill Primary School, Caversham

Recycling

People, plastic, anyone will do,
Only if you can recycle it
Like bottles but not chips.

Recycling is good because it helps the world,
You could be a hero
If you do it as well.

Brandon Lee Worth (10)
Uxendon Manor Primary School, Kenton

Deep Peace Of The Quiet Earth

We've got to get this changed,
I'll try, try and try
To get something different arranged.
There is war going on
And people are throwing litter.
What shall we really do
To make this world better?
There are diseases spreading
And people who are homeless.
We've got to put a lot of effort in
And clean up this mess.
There is a lot of pollution
And this is a big situation.
Animals are dying
So we must keep trying,
So please save the environment.

Janvi Patel (8)
Uxendon Manor Primary School, Kenton

Racism

Racism is everywhere in the world
Racism about cultures
Racism about skin colours
And racism about lots more things.

Now is the time to stop that racism
Because it is too much now
So enter a whole new world
Without any racism.

Hawa Bati (10)
Uxendon Manor Primary School, Kenton

Litter, Litter Every Day

Litter, litter every day!
Make the most of the day.
Rubbish.
Nature goes away.
Animals come along,
Eating all the rubbish all day long.
1, 2, 3 and chokes.
Litter, litter every day,
Litter is everywhere,
On the floor,
In the park,
On the pavement,
But not in the *bin!*

Vivetha Vigineswaran (10)
Uxendon Manor Primary School, Kenton

The World At War

Bang! You are dead!
Watch those guns fire!
What can I do?
If I try to stop them they will kill me!
Oh what horror!
If only they respected each other
The world will be much safer.
Eleven o'clock the clock struck
The last bomb exploded.
Thank goodness the war has ended.
No more war if everyone respects each other.

Fawaz Muhsin (10)
Uxendon Manor Primary School, Kenton

Litter

Do not throw litter
Or do not chuck rubbish
Do not put crisp packets on the floor
Or do not let dogs and cats eat crisps
And do not let them choke
Animals get ill if they choke
Do not waste food
If you eat something throw it in the bin
Please throw rubbish properly
We will not throw rubbish at people.
Save the world!

Tulsi Patel (10)
Uxendon Manor Primary School, Kenton

Litter

Litter, it's everywhere
On the road, in the garden
Up, down, all around
On the floor
Along comes an animal . . .
Eats up a bag
1, 2, 3 and chokes
One less life
Just because of one thing . . . litter
It's the small things that make a big difference.

Kelsey Pye (10)
Uxendon Manor Primary School, Kenton

Rainforest

They are really half a world away,
There's nothing we can do.
Rainforests might be too far away to kids like me and you,
They are really somewhere over there.
I may not see half the world's plants, animals and insects live
in harmony,
I know that trees are being cut faster than we know.
These trees where the creatures live,
So now where will they go?

Nyveka Sasitharan (8)
Uxendon Manor Primary School, Kenton

Suffering

Just imagine the animals suffering,
They could have lived longer except
Some people decided to ruin their homes.
Like birds they're being ruined, because the trees with nests,
Are just being cut down.
People throwing rubbish on the floor killing more animals,
How can they do it?

Katie Hostettler (10)
Uxendon Manor Primary School, Kenton

Keep Us Alive

All types of animals die every day but you don't shed a tear.
Bang here, bang there, bang everywhere
And I can't believe they are still here.
In the next ten years when I am twenty there will not be plenty
around here,
Every day I pray that some will say, hey, let's not kill today.

Michael Mason (10)
Uxendon Manor Primary School, Kenton

Wonderful Recycling

Can you recycle what you can?
Such as paper, plastic or aluminium cans.
Do you know what the advantage is?
It is that the landfill will stop growing!
Always throw the rubbish in the right bins,
It will help reduce pollution
And we will be less ill.
So please help any way you can,
Like to recycle anything you can
And you can help the world stop being polluted,
By recycling!

Sanchit Agreawal (9)
Uxendon Manor Primary School, Kenton

Animals And Extinction

Throughout the day animals are becoming extinct,
One by one they all are going.
No one's helping them,
They're all going, asking for your help.
But you're not bothering so what's the point?
Once they're gone, tears will come running by.
I'm telling the truth; it's not any lie.
So if you've got a heart
Help them *now!*
Before they've lost their heart.

Kulvinder Wariabharaj (11)
Uxendon Manor Primary School, Kenton

Join Our Team And Recycle

If you want our world to be a better place,
This is the challenge you must face.
Pick up plastic, pick up glass,
Pick up newspapers which can make the world last.
Pick up litter, it's everywhere you look.
All this rubbish can make a brand new book.
Plants are dying, they need your help.
You're the one that can give them the health.
So if you're ready give us a shout,
Join our team and there'll be *no* doubt.

Husain Kalimi (7)
Uxendon Manor Primary School, Kenton

Racism

Don't judge people by their colour or religion.
If you are racist then you are not a good friend.
If you are racist then you might hurt someone's feelings.
If you are mean to lots of people you will end up with no friends.
You will be lonely and no one will like you.
If someone is being mean to you try to ignore them
And if they are really annoying you, just walk away. Don't delay!
So please don't be racist or discriminate against someone.
Don't be mean like a big mean machine.
So remember this, *don't be racist to anyone!*

Tanzim Ahmed (10)
Uxendon Manor Primary School, Kenton

Run, Run, Run

Get away, no delay,
Here they come, run, run, run.
Bombs are dropping on the floor,
Here they come more and more.
Don't get caught up in the fun,
No fun, let's run.
More and more fired at our doors,
As fast as an eagle, as annoying as a measle.
Well wait for them to go there, here and there oh no!
Drop your guns this isn't fun,
We have rights, so please do not fight.

Uzayr Undre (9)
Uxendon Manor Primary School, Kenton

Help, Bang, Arrrgh

100,000 soldiers came and now none remain.
Bombs flying everywhere as deadly as a fiery flame.
Planes exploding, guns reloading, people dying.
Generals sighing, a thousand bullets flying.
If they carry on like this there's going to be a World War III.
For goodness sake it's only oil
And animals get hurt as well, oh what a spoil.
Yuck, what's that horrible smell?
It's the smell of people dying so stop war.

Laith Elzubaidi (10)
Uxendon Manor Primary School, Kenton

Litter Is Everywhere

Litter is everywhere.
Pick it up or animals choke when we throw.
Let the animals survive,
So why don't you put litter in the bin?
Please save the animals,
I can see litter floating away.
Please save a tree,
Please be generous.
Why don't you put litter in the right place?
If you don't it is such a waste.
Please do something,
Please save the world.

Pareena Shah (10)
Uxendon Manor Primary School, Kenton

No More War

Bang! Bang! Bang!
Bullets flying everywhere.
Bang! 'Watch out! Oh no, you're dead.'
Just watch the bazooka, shots flying everywhere.
'Argh! Attack!' No please, stop fighting.
Boom! Boom! Boom! Stop *now!*
Stop fighting for oil and respect each other!
If you do I'll give you all the oil you want!
The clock strikes 12 at night and all the soldiers ask for oil.
The war is over.

Somil Parmar (10)
Uxendon Manor Primary School, Kenton

Where Are They?

Animals are going,
Where to?
Nobody knows.
Why shoot them?
Why kill them?
What did they do to you?
You don't have a right to let them survive.
Stop lying about and get up and help.
There will be no animals left.
Pick up your litter and make them fitter.
Leave them alone *now!*

Diva Patel (10)
Uxendon Manor Primary School, Kenton

I'd Rather Be

I'd rather be thin than fat.
I'd rather be a dog than a cat.
I'd rather be happy than sad.
I'd rather be normal than mad.
I'd rather run fast than walk.
I'd rather be quiet than talk.
I'd rather be a ball than a bat.
I'd rather be a mouse than a rat.
I'd rather be a Keval than a devil.
I'd rather be a medal than a petal.

Keval Mawji (9)
Uxendon Manor Primary School, Kenton

Please Look After Them

Why kill animals?
They are just beautiful mammals.
Don't kill them for food,
That's so rude.
They think it's alright
But it's not right.
Please care about them.
They are precious as a gem.
They eat.
You kill them for meat.
Don't shoot or hunt please!

Aashni Patel (10)
Uxendon Manor Primary School, Kenton

Save Our Planet

Please keep our planet clean.
Please don't pollute it is not good.
We can walk to school instead, isn't that cool.
Look at them they just drop litter everywhere.
They don't even care, careless people.
I was just going to pick it up but somebody picks it up,
They are so good,
So there are some people who care about our planet,
So all of us should try.

Sania Mallal (9)
Uxendon Manor Primary School, Kenton

Polar Bears

Polar bears fight for the climate change
They swim 100 miles a day
Fight for food until they die
Walk on melting ice at night
Extinction is no choice to take
Save the polar bears from extinction
From now on please walk, everybody
Come on walk the extra mile.

Nimit Dodhia (9)
Uxendon Manor Primary School, Kenton

Deforestation

In the jungle the animals play happily.
The monkeys swing from tree to tree.
The birds race in the air.
The insects gossip here to there.
The trees whisper quietly.
The pond skaters skate on the pond.
The parrots a bit too fond.
That's how the jungle should be.

Now it's chopped down.
The animals scream.
That's how the jungle should not be.
There's sawdust on the ground.
The trees make no sound.

Connor Fogarty (10)
Wessex Primary School, Maidenhead

Homeless Need Help!

Think of all the people who become
Homeless in the world each day,
The people just want to hide
And cover their feelings away.

The poor people have no homes,
Nowhere to hide away,
Nowhere to protect them
When storms are coming their way.

The homeless need help
But no one seems to care.
We don't treat them fair.
We're wearing the hopes away
Of everything becoming right one day.

Why doesn't anyone care?
Why doesn't anyone realise
The work that needs to be done
To make people's lives better?

Shannon Bett (10)
Wessex Primary School, Maidenhead

Save Our World For Others!

Stop polluting, start recycling,
Stop driving, start cycling,
Stop fighting, start reciting,
Stop burgling, start gurgling,
Stop extinction, start distinction,
Start to save the world.

Wars are starting, friendships are ending,
Animals are dying, birds aren't flying,
Rainforests are burning, smoke is learning,
Please start to save the world!

Holly Johnson (11)
Wessex Primary School, Maidenhead

My Green Earth

My Earth's grass is green
And its sea is clean.
The ground is soft and hard,
With bees humming in a yard.

But this Earth is rotten to the core
And this is also caused by war.
Blood fills the plains
And everywhere is in chains.

But the world I dream of,
Is filled with happiness from above
And clean air fills everywhere
And people are spared.

But this Earth is not green,
Everything is mean
And not a single bean can grow,
It's just like below.

But the green world
Is hurled
In a green way,
Nothing ever goes astray.

People of the world hear a plea,
Please recycle,
Please stop the pollution,
Please stop this madness
Or this world will never become green
And everything will be extinct . . .
Forever . . .

Please help *the world.*

Matthew Sadlier (11)
Wessex Primary School, Maidenhead

Young Writers - The Big Green Poetry Machine London & The Home Counties Poets **115**

End Racism

We all must bring our
Racism to an end.
A message to all,
I long to send.

You really hurt
Others in life,
When you're
Racist to them.

The colours of the world
All join as one.
For the Lord is our shepherd
And we as His son.

Christ made all man
In the likes of Him.
People are dying
Of the words they hear.
People cry wondering
Why?
So please let us all
End racism.

Aiysha Ali (11)
Wessex Primary School, Maidenhead

Litter

Litter is very bad,
It makes me really sad.
I hope this will be put to a stop,
Otherwise I will burst and pop.

It hurts animals, it hurts me,
Why don't you just let us all free?
Please take care of our world,
Make the Earth clear and bowed.

Molly Miles (11)
Wessex Primary School, Maidenhead

Endangered Animals

Animals everywhere,
Watch them go,
They won't be here for long,
People are killing them
For money and just for fun.

Run and help before there's just one,
Because this can't be undone,
Anyone can help even you,
Just make sure you don't harm them too.

Louise Clarke (11)
Wessex Primary School, Maidenhead

Earth

E arth is precious
A place to live
R ound and round it goes on its axis
T he Earth is in danger
H elp us save it!

Shannon Hawkins (11)
Wessex Primary School, Maidenhead

Let's Help, Be Green

Start a revolution, make a solution
Stop cutting trees, make a breeze
Stop fighting, start reciting

Stop extinction, despair distinction
Animals are dying, people are crying
Rainforest growing, trees are going

Wars starting, people carting
Stop driving, start cycling.

Andrew Newlyn (10)
Wessex Primary School, Maidenhead

Wanted: Humans For Destroying Earth!

Danger is surrounding the place
Everyone's got a sad face
Destruction is our enemy
What's the poor Earth to do?

Animals are getting killed all the time
Robbers and murderers keep making crimes
Fire setting our world in agony
What's the poor Earth to do?

Rubbish is littering the world all around
Driving makes petrol kill plants on the ground
Poisonous gases surrounding the air
What's the poor Earth to do?

But we can help make a difference
We can help make it alright
We can save our homes from danger
And in the darkness, put in a light.

We can recycle all our rubbish
Instead of just throwing it to the floor
We can give money to charities
So people have a home once more.

Sakshi Raizada (11)
Wessex Primary School, Maidenhead

Stay Clean, Be Green

Look out for a green cleaning machine,
Recycle trash you might get cash.

I was walking down the street, there was a can,
I put it in the bin, I felt like a man.

If there's a sign saying don't litter you will stay fitter,
If you don't pick up your litter you could be a skitter.

Joshua Belton (11)
Wessex Primary School, Maidenhead

Pollution Isn't Pointless

Pollution is everywhere
In the air today,
Turning smiley faces
To a face of dismay.

Greenhouse gases
Killing the world around,
You cannot hear the moans and groans
Of the Earth being drowned.

Clouds of smoke and acid rain
Take over our sunny days,
Fires and earthquakes
Making houses become ablaze.

When we finally see
What our world has become,
We will soon realise
Our world is looking glum.

Our children will want to know
What happened in the past,
We can only look a shade of red
And tell them what happened last.

Julia Reid (11)
Wessex Primary School, Maidenhead

Orang-Utans

Orang-utans lonely in the trees
Losing their homes, help them please
Men with machines dangerous and loud
Cutting down trees for roads and houses
Take your heads out of the clouds
Say stop before they die
We don't want it on our conscience to hear their last sigh
When they become extinct
It will be because we didn't *stop* and *think!*

Zakhia Hussain (11)
Wessex Primary School, Maidenhead

Litter

Litter makes me really sad,
Dropping it is very bad.
It's bad for plants, it's bad for me,
Not to mention it's bad for the sea.

I can't bear the horrible thought
Of a rabbit getting caught
In a beer can, in a box,
Getting trapped then eaten by a fox.

Did you know about a bin?
That's what you put your rubbish in.
It's good for plants, it's good for me
And don't forget it's good for the sea.

Kimberley Bradfield (11)
Wessex Primary School, Maidenhead

Rainforests!

What can you see?
Animals, plants or litter

What can you hear?
People walking through the woods
And cutting the trees down or animals making sounds?

What can you smell?
Pollution from cars, fresh flowers or all the different kinds of gases?

What can you feel?
The air brushing through your hair
Or old trees that got cut down brushing on your legs?

Hou-Yee Cheung (11)
Wessex Primary School, Maidenhead

Recycling

If you are green by recycling
It saves the world like cycling.
Bags, bottles and paper too,
If you recycle the green thing will be you.

If you recycle it will be cool,
If you do you will be the king of the school.
Pick up your rubbish and off you trot,
Where you picked up rubbish, is now a cleaner spot.

Save the day and be good,
What you do, it just could.
Leave the trees, leave the wood,
Everyone else would be misunderstood.

Ross Moloney (11)
Wessex Primary School, Maidenhead

Endangered Animals

The temperature is rising,
Here and everywhere,
It's too much for the animals,
Just like the polar bear.

The ice is melting,
Their lives are fading away,
If we don't help they'll just be a memory for another day,
Let them live, let them stay.

Reanne Hawkins (11)
Wessex Primary School, Maidenhead

Green As Green Can Be

I'm gonna tell you something,
Very, very true.
A very important story,
About me and you.

In the Earth's atmosphere
There is a lot to learn,
About stuff like greenhouse gases
And even a garden urn.

What I'm trying to tell you,
Is that we need to be
Very, very tidy
And very, very green.

Turn off lights and TVs,
Toasters, kettles too.
Switch off everything,
But don't switch off you.

I hope this situation
Has got into your mind,
Like being nice to plants
And to animals be kind.

Grace Perfect (11)
Wessex Primary School, Maidenhead

Save, Save, Save Our Energy

Save, save, save,
No more burning coal and oil,
No more burying rubbish in the soil,
Save, save, save.

Grow, grow, grow,
Plant the trees or they will die,
Then the new trees will come and say hi,
Grow, grow, grow.

Erin Harley & Jessie Haines (10)
Wessex Primary School, Maidenhead

Nobody Cares . . .

P eople never think,
O nly about them.
L ook world,
L et's be green!
U nderestimating our world's power,
T he world will exact a toll.
I t is bigger than you can imagine,
O nly we can stop it . . .
N ow!

O nly us,
N o more help.

E ating away at the Earth's resources,
A ll we can do is watch.
R eally nobody is winning,
T hough people think they are.
H ow could we let this happen?

Robert Pratley (11)
Wessex Primary School, Maidenhead

The Trees

The trees start to grow,
Bark starts to emerge strong.

But it gets cut down,
Next it comes again.

Swings in the air happily,
But we are killing them.

Trees cry and scream to be rescued,
Save me! But nobody helps.

The trees turn into paper,
It turns thin and soft.

I am saving the trees,
Now it is your turn.

Saima Ali (10)
Wessex Primary School, Maidenhead

A Thousand Trees

A thousand trees are cut down every day
To make the paper you just throw away.

Act now, recycle paper
Or you'll become a rubbish monster.

A tree is a living thing
Why are you being so mean?

Soon all the trees will disappear
That's what I really fear.

All this deforestation makes no oxygen
Makes me lose my concentration.

Act now, let the trees survive
And you'll get a grand prize.

The prize is a world unknown
But you will never know unless you start saving the trees.

Oliver Crockett & Oliver Mulley (10)
Wessex Primary School, Maidenhead

Rainforests

R ubbish in our rainforests
A nimals are losing their homes
I nvisible sights
N o one will ever care
F orest frogs are dying out
O range orang-utans are rare
R emember to stay calm
E verything deserves a life
S oon every rainforest will be gone
T oday things need to change
S o let's make a difference.

Heather Armstrong (11)
Wessex Primary School, Maidenhead

Save The World

Littering, littering
All on the floor,
It makes me angry,
Don't do it anymore.

Pollution, pollution,
From factories and cars,
If we carry on,
We don't get very far.

Extinction, extinction,
Animals disappearing every day,
Please don't shoot,
They will all fade away.

Rainforests, rainforests,
Paper comes from its trees,
Don't get rid of the rainforests,
We need its oxygen to breathe.

Alicia Carrington (10)
Wessex Primary School, Maidenhead

Rainforest Blues

R escue the rainforest
A home for some
I need you to listen
N o animals you see
F amilies of monkeys scared and weak
O rang-utans and toucans are shocked and vulnerable
R ead this poem and feel emotion and change this world
E ducate everybody and tell them this tragedy
S ome won't listen, some don't care, let's change their minds today
T hink where they're gonna go
S ay something, be a survivor!

Daisy Fox
Wessex Primary School, Maidenhead

Our Creatures

We do have creatures
Becoming extinct by day
And hunted by night.

We do have creatures,
The white rhino is hunted
For its lovely horn.

We do have creatures,
The tiger is in slavery,
Travelling around.

We do have creatures
Big and small living here too,
So notice them soon!

Hannah Higgins
Wessex Primary School, Maidenhead

Rainforests

Do not cut the trees,
You are destroying the animals' families,
They have no home
And they are going to moan.

Scientists, scientists
Think of a way to make paper
Without using our precious trees,
Use your brains,
Use them now!

Stop cutting down the trees,
Leave the animals and their families,
Think now!
Come on, please think now!

Jack Brinsden (11)
Wessex Primary School, Maidenhead

Sad World

Sad world
Death for all
I hear screaming
I'm scared
Please stop
Burning houses
Blood everywhere
People dying
Big explosions
Buildings falling
Taking people away
Arms lost
Help us
Oh please
No food
No homes
Nothing at all
Gun shots
Bang, bang!

Harry Simmonds
Wessex Primary School, Maidenhead

Extinction

Speed killers
Ivory takers
Quiet watchers
Extinction makers
Time wasters
Screaming chasers
Animal losers
Restless creatures
Animal killers
Bang, bang
Animal eaters
Please stop.

Catherine Styles (11)
Wessex Primary School, Maidenhead

Why? Why? Why?

Litter sitting by the street,
    Why? Why? Why?
A pigeon dying in a Pepsi can,
    Why? Why? Why?
A cigarette thrown on a blackberry bush,
    Why? Why? Why?
The bush is in flames and is burning fast,
    Why? Why? Why?
'Cause people really do not care,
    Why? Why? Why?
Nobody knows, to be honest,
    But I really do care.

Leyan Yucel (11)
Wessex Primary School, Maidenhead

The World

The litter gets thrown on the ground
Which then hurts the animals which makes them frown.
Every year 100,000 dolphins are killed.
Recycle, recycle stop the animals getting hurt.
Birds fly in the air, trees growing, putting oxygen in the air.
Make the world green, you can grow a bean,
To save the amount of pollution just bring a can of beans.

Hannah Risk (11)
Wessex Primary School, Maidenhead

The Greenie Poem

If you stop dropping cans
There might be more greener lands.
Litter harms me and you,
So think about what you do.
Now after you've dropped a sweet wrapper,
Pick it up and do your part for the environment.

Adam Garston (10)
Wessex Primary School, Maidenhead

Rainforests

Rainforests are going.
Air is going.
Ice is melting.
Nothing is here anymore.
Fish are hiding to survive.
Oxygen is going
Rising into an oiled wave.
Swimming in an oil slick.
Terrified fish all alone.
Swimming in oil slick makes me sick.

Rachel Hibberd (11)
Wessex Primary School, Maidenhead

Pollution

B ad
I nsults
G reen

G o green
R emember
E arth
E veryone
N o pollution.

Aicha Traore (10)
Wessex Primary School, Maidenhead

Litter

L eave our planet alone
I magine a world with no animals or plants
T reat the Earth with love
T ry and care
E ncourage others to recycle
R espect the world.

Jenny Barnard (11)
Wessex Primary School, Maidenhead

Animals

People don't know they're there
Some people don't really care

Animals are dying one by one
Some people care that they're gone

One of those people includes me
I love animals for me to see.

Emma Brown (11)
Wessex Primary School, Maidenhead

The Sloth

A sloth is lazy like Chelsea my sister
A sloth is slow like a snail
A sloth is big like my friend Chris
A sloth can swim like a dog
A sloth has nails shaped like bananas
A sloth has fur so soft and smooth
A sloth sleeps like Sara my sister
A sloth has beady eyes
A sloth is kind and cute.

Kallum Harris
Wessex Primary School, Maidenhead

Save The Water

Save the water
Not just a quarter.

Think of more than just one kid
Think they have no water, place a bid!

Take too much out of the rivers
It gives some people the shivers.

Declan Feltimo (10)
Wessex Primary School, Maidenhead

Destroying Our Beautiful World

Destroying all the habitats from frogs to the forest cats
Cutting down the tall dry trees littering those clear blue seas
Killing those poor animals to sell their skins in the shopping malls
Taking away their homes, leaving them to moan and groan
How long will it take for us all to learn?
By then the world will be all dark and burnt!

Dylan Brownlie
Wessex Primary School, Maidenhead

Save The Planet

Pollution, pollution, tins and cans,
Too many people using their vans.

Fruit and veg being wasted,
Worms and creatures want it tasted.

No more chopping down the trees,
Animals need their precious leaves.

Now that you know what to do,
So save the planet you know you want to.

Rebecca Burman (10)
West Horndon Primary School, Brentwood

My Smelly Lane

My smelly lane is purple and green,
It smells so bad there is nothing to be seen.
Last time an animal came to my lane
It shrieked and it fell and it never woke again.
If you see someone polluting a lane
Please try to stop them from dumping again.

Shaun Duggan (9)
West Horndon Primary School, Brentwood

Rainforest

R educe, reuse, recycle
A nimals are dying
I nappropriate use of resources
N utrients are being taken
F orgive us for what we have done
O zone layer getting damaged
R eplace what is taken
E ndangered species need your help
S ave the day
T oday have a lot of fun.

Phoebe Hardcastle (11)
West Horndon Primary School, Brentwood

Save It!

S ave your planet!
A nimals need your help.
V arious things are destroying our planet.
E nergy is what you need to start making a difference.

I t is just small things that can make a big difference.
T ake your time saving the world!

Daisy Bird (10)
West Horndon Primary School, Brentwood

Pick Up Litter

L itter is not supposed to go on the streets
I n the recycling bin the litter goes
T ell everyone you meet
T ell everyone you know
E veryone recycle
R emember this, come on, let's go.

Amba Davies (9)
West Horndon Primary School, Brentwood

Eco-Friendly

Here are your favourite tips,
We will help you not to mix,
It's really not that hard,
The bins really aren't that far.

Keep your apples and your pears,
It really shows that you can care,
Now you've listened to my tips,
I really hope it's got you recycling quick.

Toby Lewis-Burrell (11)
West Horndon Primary School, Brentwood

Animals In Danger

Animals are dying
As I speak I am crying
Animals are in danger
Because of terrifying rangers
Tigers are so rare
As they are being hunted for their hair
Save the animals that's all we've got
We have not got a lot.

Kiera Herbert (10)
West Horndon Primary School, Brentwood

Pick Up Litter

Pick up litter, pick up litter,
Save the world today.
Put your litter in the bin.
Help animals by putting a beer bottle in the bin.
If you don't put it in the bin the animals will die.
Hear the animals say thank you,
Thank you,
Everyone will be happy.

Emily Monk (7)
West Horndon Primary School, Brentwood

Don't Cut Our Family Tree

I'm a lady lion, leave me be,
Don't cut down our family tree.
My little baby cub, now has no home.
You've left him, he's all alone.
The last I heard was a scream and yelp,
My baby boy was crying for *help!*
You nasty humans, I ask you why?
Explain yourselves, go on just try.
I'm a lady lion leave me be,
Don't cut down our family tree.

Jordan Shelvey (9)
West Horndon Primary School, Brentwood

Recycle Machine

R ecycling helps the Earth
E arth is where we live
C ompost is all our food waste
Y ou and me could help
C ountries can be killed
L akes are being destroyed
E asy things can be done!

Katie Smith (10)
West Horndon Primary School, Brentwood

Animals

A penguin got killed.
N o one was in the field.
I saw an insect getting squashed.
M y monkey was on the bop.
A tiger was bitten.
L ove is the word.
S o stop.

Antoinette Pieri (7)
West Horndon Primary School, Brentwood

Recycling

Take your glass bottles, paper and pots
To a recycling tip.
It would be a good trip
And don't throw it away.
If you throw it away
It will rot and go to waste.

If you have a picnic
Never ever ever
Just leave it on its own.
If you want to save the world
Recycle today.

Anya Carter (7)
West Horndon Primary School, Brentwood

Pick Up Litter

Pick up litter,
Pick up litter,
Save the world today.
Put your litter in the bin
And hear the animals say,
You've saved the world
And all the land.
It has made a lot of difference.

Chloe Oughton (9)
West Horndon Primary School, Brentwood

Earth

E nergy has been getting wasted.
A nimals are dying as we speak.
R ain is not here.
T he planet is suffering.
H elp it now!

Jack Simon & Jo Nann (10)
West Horndon Primary School, Brentwood

We've Got To Save The Rainforest

We've got to save the rainforests,
We're chopping it all down.
Please try and recycle paper,
We're really all such clowns.

It's really, really worrying
How much wood we are using.
Why do we need so much?
It really is confusing.

Now we need to recycle paper
And other things like wood.
If only we could do this more,
Save the rainforests we could.

We've got to save the rainforests,
We'll stop chopping it down.
We will recycle paper,
Then we won't be bigger clowns.

Reece Carter (9)
West Horndon Primary School, Brentwood

Rubbish

R euse everything you can
U nderstand what is wrong
B elieve we can change the world
B efore we think about recycling see if you can reuse
I mportant things like the world have lives as well as us
S olar panels are good for the environment
H elp the world heal.

Matthew Scammell (8)
West Horndon Primary School, Brentwood

Pollution

Pollution, pollution, pollution everywhere,
Pollution in the ground, pollution in the air,
Pollution, pollution, pollution in the sea,
Killing all the fishes with oil and mercury.
There are many ways to stop it, there's much that you can do,
Reduce your carbon footprint, reduce your heating too,
Leave your car at home for once and use your own two feet,
Throw away your rubbish, don't drop it on the street,
Or better still, recycle, don't chuck it all away,
Get back to nature and grow your five a day.
Pollution, pollution, pollution must end,
This is our Earth, it's for us to defend.

Annabel Jarvis (10)
West Horndon Primary School, Brentwood

Earth

E nergy, save it by turning off lights.
A nimals are endangered like polar bears because the North Pole
is melting.
R ecycle, reduce and reuse.
T rees are being dug up.
H ouse, by turning off lights when they are not being useful.

Jack Little (11)
West Horndon Primary School, Brentwood

Recycle

Recycle, don't throw away,
You're endangering the environment, have a thought today.
Don't throw cans in rivers, throw it in the recycling bin,
We need them, we will win.

George Wise (8)
West Horndon Primary School, Brentwood

The Big Green World

Come on everybody,
We need to start this job.
The trees are better in the woods,
So don't chop down your logs.
When I look at the forest it looks so natural.

Recycle pots,
Recycle cans,
Recycle everything you can.
It's better than the landfill site because it is a dump,
So don't put your things in the dump.

Melanie Sedge (9)
West Horndon Primary School, Brentwood

Pick Up Litter

Pick up litter,
Pick up litter,
Save the world today.
Help the animals in their homes
And put the litter away.
Hear the animals say,
Thank you, thank you,
For helping us to make new homes
And keeping the litter away
And most of all,
Keep it away!

Alex Oughton (10)
West Horndon Primary School, Brentwood

War On The World

The cries of men dying,
While Tommy guns are firing.
Machine guns slaughtering men
Ten by ten.

Tanks move but get stuck
In French blood soaked muck.
Planes fly and spy
But get shot down and die.

Why is there war?
It changes community law.
Why are people angry and sad?
Because killed are lads and dads.

James Hemington (11)
Wildridings Primary School, Bracknell

Weather

Rain, sun, wind, snow,
All good, that's what you think you know.

Flood, drought, hurricane, avalanche,
All enough to break a branch.

Houses, lives, feelings, health,
Fighting these uses up wealth.

So please give money,
Give it to charity.
Money can repair damages,
Instead of using bandages.

Alice Morgan (11)
Wildridings Primary School, Bracknell

As The Guns Fire Here And There

As the guns fire here and there,
Death and disgrace everywhere.
You can't escape the dying faith,
What has happened to the human race?

As all the colour fades away,
The whole world turns to grey.
As the time goes by,
More and more people die.

A family sits with their heads in their hands,
But no matter what happens the war still stands.
War is far worse than bad,
People throwing away what they had.

Souls resting in the grave,
Families for life they crave.
As they look back on their happy days,
In the ground the body lays.

All the families move on,
The war still has not gone.
More and more people fight,
It doesn't end day or night.

As the guns fire here and there . . .

Connor Langham (11)
Wildridings Primary School, Bracknell

Pollution

Acid mutation
All over the nation.

Litter flying,
Animals choking and dying.

Cars, vehicles, factories too,
Gases released by people like you.

Tyler Jones (10)
Wildridings Primary School, Bracknell

Go Green!

If there's litter on the ground,
Recycle it all year round,
Do it with bottles and bits
And you could watch TV for ten minutes!
Pollution is a very bad thing,
So go outside and sing,
Factories stop working
And birds start flying.
Extinct and threatened animals
Killed by hunters who don't obey the rules,
Rainforests chopped down flat,
That ruins animals' habitats.
As you can see we're destroying the planet,
But there is still much more time to prevent it.
The Earth will forgive us, it knows we're not mean,
So people of the Earth shout out . . .
Go green!

Kenesha Barracliffe (11)
Wildridings Primary School, Bracknell

Our World

Animals, pollution, gases too,
Extinct animals saved by the zoo.

Cake wrappers, cans, tins and more,
It's all there, so what are we waiting for?

Pick up your rubbish, litter and cans
And use your legs instead of vans.

Be eco-friendly recycle and more
And don't kill wild animals because it's against the law.

Abigail Harris (11)
Wildridings Primary School, Bracknell

Planet Changer

I will save my planet . . .
By throwing my chocolate wrapper in the bin,
By recycling my old newspapers
And by destroying all plastic bags.

I will help my planet . . .
By protesting on cutting down rainforests,
To stop extinction.
By keeping clean and free of bugs,
So nobody's ill.

I will protect my planet . . .
By killing war and welcoming peace,
Walking away from pollution
And by helping the unlucky, homeless people.

I will change my planet . . .
By encouraging children to join in
On these planet converting actions.
Our planet will be a better place
If we cooperate together.

Zara Ryan (9)
Woolton Hill Primary School, Newbury

Disease

D iseases cause you to be ill,
 I f you're lucky the doctor will give you a pill.
S ome countries have dirty water.
E very person can help by splitting their pocket money into
                                                   a quarter.
A ll of you could make a difference.
S hare your money and begin the clearance.
E veryone can make this world a better place to be for you and me.

Ruby Hornsby (9)
Woolton Hill Primary School, Newbury

War

People fighting for their lives,
Guns, swords and knives.
War leaders,
Battle bleeders,
Have all gone to war.
The events which came
Will never be the same.
Royalty,
Loyalty,
Have all gone to war,
Will this go on forever?
Could we pull ourselves together,
Sergeants, lieutenants, ourselves?

Edwin Edwards (10)
Woolton Hill Primary School, Newbury

Mountain Gorilla

I live on mountains by the trees,
I still feel a chilly breeze.
Along one day there they came
And locked me up in ball and chain.

I only felt the pain come
When they shot me with a gun.
Then I felt so very queasy
And people think my life is easy.

Thomas Hall (10)
Woolton Hill Primary School, Newbury

Young Writers Information

We hope you have enjoyed reading this
book - and that you will continue to enjoy it
in the coming years.

If you like reading and writing poetry drop
us a line, or give us a call, and we'll send
you a free information pack.

Alternatively if you would like to order
further copies of this book or any of our
other titles, then please give us a call or
log onto our website at
www.youngwriters.co.uk

**Young Writers Information
Remus House
Coltsfoot Drive
Woodston
Peterborough
PE2 9JX**

(01733) 890066